The Supporters Guide to Non-League Football 1994

EDITOR
John Robinson

Second Edition

CONTENTS

Foreword 3
The Pyramid 4
GM/Vauxhall Conference 5-26
Diadora League - Premier Division 27-48
Diadora League Divisions 1-3 49-51
Northern Premier League - Premier Division 52-73
Northern Premier League - Division 1 74
Northern Counties (East) League - Premier Division 75
Northern League - Division 1 76
Bass North Western Counties League - Division 1 77
Beazer Homes League - Premier Division 78-99
Beazer Homes League - Midland & Southern Divisions 100-101
Statistics for the 1992/93 Season 102-105
Final League Tables for the 1992/93 Season 106-107
Non-League Publications 108-109
Advertisements 110-112

British Library Cataloguing in Publication Data
A catalogue record for this book is available from the British Library
ISBN 0-947808-27-2

Copyright © 1993; SOCCER BOOK PUBLISHING LTD. (0472-696226)
72, St. Peters' Avenue, Cleethorpes, Sth. Humberside, DN35 8HU, England

All rights are reserved. No part of this publication may be reproduced, stored into a retrieval system or transmitted, in any form or by any means, electronic, mechanical, photocopying, recording, or otherwise, without the prior written permission of Soccer Book Publishing Ltd.

The Publishers, and the Football Clubs itemised are unable to accept liability for any loss, damage or injury caused by error or inaccuracy in the information published in this guide.

Printed by Adlard Print & Typesetting Services, The Old School, The Green, Ruddington, Notts. NG11 6HH

FOREWORD

Following our successful launch of the separate Supporters' Guide to Non-League Football last year, we have maintained a similar format for this edition with completely updated information. Where possible we have now also included a contact phone number other than the ground number and road directions have been amended.

Although we use the term 'Child' for concessionary prices, this practically always, is the price charged to Senior Citizens also. We welcome comments from readers as to items which they feel should be included in future editions.

Our thanks go to the numerous club officials who have assisted us in the compilation of the information contained in this guide and also to Michael Robinson (page layouts), Chris Ambler (photos) and Darren Kirk (cover artwork) for the part that they have played. We are also indebted to the secretary's of the various leagues for providing statistical information and extensive support.

In addition, we wish to thank Tony Williams of the major Non-League football monthly TEAM TALK for the information about The Pyramid which appears on page 4.

Supporters of Football League Clubs, Scottish Football & Welsh Football and should note that we publish THE SUPPORTERS' GUIDE TO PREMIER & FOOTBALL LEAGUE CLUBS - 1994 EDITION (£4.99), THE SUPPORTERS' GUIDE TO SCOTTISH FOOTBALL 1994 (£4.99) and THE SUPPORTERS' GUIDE TO WELSH FOOTBALL 1994 (£4.99) all of which are available, post free, from the address opposite.

Finally, we would like to wish our readers a happy and safe spectating season.

John Robinson
EDITOR

THE PYRAMID

The concept of the 'Pyramid' has invigorated Non-League football over the past decade, especially now that the G.M. Vauxhall Conference champions are promoted automatically to the Third Division of the Football League. Instead of being involved in local isolated competitions, clubs can now see themselves in a national context.

The G.M. Vauxhall Conference is the top rung of the Pyramid. The second rung accommodates the Diadora, Beazer Homes and Northern Premier Leagues, and these three competitions can be seen as the top rung in each of three regional branches that are fully explained below.

Whilst not common, it is not unheard of for clubs to switch from one branch of the Pyramid to another, especially in 'grey areas' where clubs are torn between two branches. Typical examples have been Boston switching from the Websters Central Midlands to the United Counties League, Viking Sports moving from Hellenic to the Dan-Air, and Wigston Fields and Barlestone St. Giles leaving the Leicestershire League for the Influence Combination.

THE DIADORA (ISTHMIAN) BRANCH

There are four leagues officially recognised as feeders to the Diadora Third Division; the Dan-Air, the Essex Senior, the Campri South Midlands (two divisions), and the London Spartan (three divisions). Because the Diadora has four divisions, a club progressing from one of its feeders would need to win two more promotions than a like club in either the Beazer Branch or Northern Premier branch. The Diadora Section is the most flexible in that the additional feeders are not rigidly tied to any one of the leagues above them.

BEAZER HOMES (SOUTHERN) BRANCH

This is the broadest of the three branches. There are no fewer than nine leagues officially feeding the Southern and Midland Divisions of the Beazer, and as for the most part these leagues have promotion/relegation arrangements with local leagues, this is arguably the most complete section of the Pyramid. Over the past couple of seasons, the Beazer Homes League has tightened up its ground facilities requirements, so promotion within the League and from its feeders has not been automatic. The nine feeders are also introducing strict facilities codes; the Jewson Wessex, Jewson Eastern and Great Mills League all insist on Premier Division grounds being floodlit, and the United Counties and Unijet Sussex Leagues will follow suit shortly.

NORTHERN PREMIER BRANCH

In 1991, the Northern League joined the Bass North West Counties and the Northern Counties (East) Leagues as a third official feeder to the Northern Premier League Division One. This development has had the effect of incorporating the North East in the Pyramid structure because two of the area's prominent competitions, the Northern Alliance and the Vaux Wearside League, have negotiated to become official feeder to the Northern League. The Northern Premier branch contains a very contentious 'grey area'; the East Midlands/South Yorkshire region. The Whitbread County, West Yorks and West Riding Leagues slot in under the Northern Counties (East) League, but the Notts. Alliance, Central Midlands and Leicestershire Senior Leagues are torn between the Beazer and Northern Premier branches, and therefore remain outside the official Pyramid.

ALTRINCHAM FC

Founded: 1903
Limited Company: 1921
Former Name(s): None
Nickname: 'The Robins'
Ground: Moss Lane, Altrincham, Greater Manchester WA15 8AP
Record Attendance: 10,275 (February 1925)

Colours: Shirts - Red and White Stripes
Shorts - Black
Telephone No.: (061) 928-1045
Daytime Phone No.: (061) 928-1045
Pitch Size: 115 × 70yds
Ground Capacity: 3,500
Seating Capacity: 1,000

GENERAL INFORMATION
Supporters Club Administrator: -
Address: -
Telephone Number: -
Car Parking: Adjacent
Coach Parking: By Police Direction
Nearest Railway Station: Altrincham (5 minutes walk)
Nearest Bus Station: Altrincham
Club Shop:
Opening Times: Matchdays Only
Telephone No.: (061) 928-1045
Postal Sales: Yes
Nearest Police Station: Dunham Road, Altrincham
Police Force: Greater Manchester
Police Telephone No.: (061) 855-5050

GROUND INFORMATION
Away Supporters' Entrances: Chequers End Turnstiles
Away Supporters' Sections: Chequers End of Ground

DISABLED SUPPORTERS INFORMATION
Wheelchairs: Accommodated
Disabled Toilets: None
The Blind: No Special Facilities

ADMISSION INFO (1993/94 PRICES)
Adult Standing: £4.00
Adult Seating: £5.00
Child Standing: £2.00
Child Seating: £2.50
Programme Price: £1.00
FAX Number: (061) 926-9934

```
              POPULAR SIDE
      ┌─────────────────────────┐
GOLF  │                         │ CHEQUERS
ROAD  │                         │   END
 END  │                         │  (Away)
      └─────────────────────────┘
              MAIN STAND
              MOSS LANE
```

Travelling Supporters Information:
Routes: Exit M56 junction 7 following signs Hale and Altrincham. Through 1st set of traffic lights and take 3rd right - Westminster Road and continue into Moss Lane. Ground on right.

BATH CITY FC

Founded: 1889
Former Name(s): None
Nickname: 'City'
Ground: Twerton Park, Bath   BA2 1DB
Record Attendance: 18,020 (1960)

Colours: Shirts - Black & White Stripes
Shorts - Black
Telephone No.: (0225) 423087
Daytime Phone No.: (0225) 423087
Pitch Size: 112 × 80yds
Ground Capacity: 9,899
Seating Capacity: 1,004

GENERAL INFORMATION
Supporters Club Administrator: Mr. P. Cater
Address: c/o Club
Telephone Number: (0225) 313247
Car Parking: 150 spaces at Ground
Coach Parking: Avon Street, Bath
Nearest Railway Station: Bath Spa (1.5 miles)
Nearest Bus Station: Avon Street, Bath
Club Shop:
Opening Times: Matchdays Only
Telephone No.: (0225) 423087
Postal Sales: Yes
Nearest Police Station: Bath (1.5 miles)
Police Force: Avon & Somerset
Police Telephone No.: (0225) 444343

GROUND INFORMATION
Away Supporters' Entrances: Bristol End
Away Supporters' Sections: Bristol End

DISABLED SUPPORTERS INFORMATION
Wheelchairs: Accommodated by Arrangement - Main Stand
Disabled Toilets: Yes
The Blind: Commentaries by Arrangement

ADMISSION INFO (1993/94 PRICES)
Adult Standing: £4.00
Adult Seating: £5.50
Child Standing: £3.00
Child Seating: £4.00
Programme Price: £1.00
FAX Number: (0225) 481391

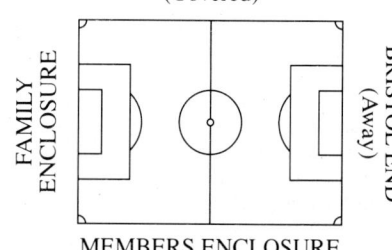

Travelling Supporters Information:
Routes: Take the A36 into Bath City Centre. Follow along Pulteney Road then right into Claverton Street and along Lower Bristol Road (A36). Left under railway (1.5 miles) into Twerton High Street and ground on left.

BROMSGROVE ROVERS FC

Founded: 1885
Former Name(s): None
Nickname: 'The Rovers'
Ground: Victoria Ground, Birmingham Road, Bromsgrove, Worcs
Record Attendance: 7,563 (1957/58)

Colours: Shirts - Green & White Stripes
Shorts - Black
Telephone No.: (0527) 76949
Daytime Phone No.: (0527) 79649
Pitch Size: 110 × 72yds
Ground Capacity: 4,800
Seating Capacity: 372

GENERAL INFORMATION
Supporters Club Administrator: Chris Fox
Address: c/o Club
Telephone Number: (0527) 76949
Car Parking: At Ground (200 cars)
Coach Parking: By Police Direction
Nearest Railway Station: Bromsgrove (1.5 miles)
Nearest Bus Station: 500 yards
Club Shop: Yes
Opening Times: Weekdays 9.00-2.00pm and also all home matches
Telephone No.: (0527) 76949
Postal Sales: Yes
Nearest Police Station: Bromsgrove Central
Police Force: West Mercia
Police Telephone No.: (0527) 579888

GROUND INFORMATION
Away Supporters' Entrances: -
Away Supporters' Sections: Segregation not usual

DISABLED SUPPORTERS INFORMATION
Wheelchairs: Accommodated
Disabled Toilets: None
The Blind: No Special Facilities

ADMISSION INFO (1993/94 PRICES)
Adult Standing: £4.50
Adult Seating: £5.50
Child Standing: £2.50
Child Seating: £3.50
Programme Price: £1.00
FAX Number: (0527) 76949

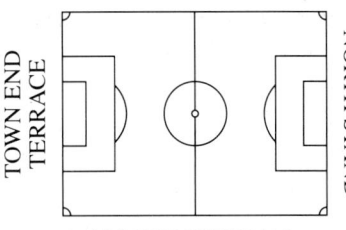

Travelling Supporters Information:
Routes: From the North: Exit the M42 at junction 1 and follow the A38 towards Bromsgrove. Once in Bromsgrove, at the traffic lights follow Town Centre signs. Victoria Ground is approximately 2 minutes away next to Clark's Motor Services on the right hand side; From the South: Exit the M5 at junction 4 onto the A38. Then as above.

DAGENHAM & REDBRIDGE FC

Founded: 1992
Former Name(s): Formed by merging of Dagenham FC & Redbridge Forest FC
Nickname: 'The Reds'
Ground: Victoria Road, Dagenham, Essex, RM10 7XL
Record Attendance: 7,100 (1967)

Colours: Shirts - Red
Shorts - Blue
Telephone No.: (081) 592-1549/593-7070
Daytime Phone No.: (0277) 363103
Pitch Size: 112 × 72yds
Ground Capacity: 7,500
Seating Capacity: 720

GENERAL INFORMATION
Supporters Club Administrator: Richard White
Address: -
Telephone Number: (0268) 418564
Car Parking: Car Park at Ground
Coach Parking: Car Park at Ground
Nearest Railway Station: Dagenham East (5 minutes walk)
Nearest Bus Station: Romford
Club Shop: At Ground
Opening Times: Matchdays Only
Telephone No.: -
Postal Sales: Yes
Nearest Police Station: Dagenham East
Police Force: Metropolitan
Police Telephone No.: -

GROUND INFORMATION
Away Supporters' Entrances: Pondfield Road
Away Supporters' Sections: Pondfield End

DISABLED SUPPORTERS INFORMATION
Wheelchairs: Accommodated
Disabled Toilets: Yes
The Blind: No commentaries but assistance given

ADMISSION INFO (1993/94 PRICES)
Adult Standing: £4.50
Adult Seating: £6.50
Child Standing: £2.50
Child Seating: £6.50
Programme Price: £1.00
FAX Number: (081) 593-7227

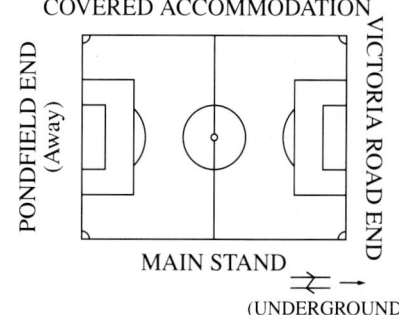

Travelling Supporters Information:
Routes: From West: Take A118 or A12 (Eastern Avenue) into Dagenham turning right into Whalebone Lane. Branch left at Sports Arena into Wood Lane, then Rainham Road. After 0.5 mile turn right into Victoria Road for Ground; From East: Take A118 or A12 (Eastern Avenue) into Dagenham turning left into Whalebone Lane (then as West); From North: Take B174 from Romford straight into Whalebone Lane (then as West from Eastern Avenue).

DOVER ATHLETIC FC

Founded: 1983
Former Name(s): None
Nickname: 'Lillywhites'
Ground: Crabble Athletic Ground, Lewisham Road, River, Dover, Kent
Record Attendance: 4,035

Colours: Shirts - White
Shorts - Black
Telephone No.: (0304) 822373
Daytime Phone No.: (0227) 769708 (evenings)
Pitch Size: 110 × 75yds
Ground Capacity: 6,500
Seating Capacity: 750

GENERAL INFORMATION
Supporters Club Administrator: Chris Graves
Address: Dover Athletic Supporters Club, 4 Albert Road, Canterbury, Kent
Telephone Number: (0227) 769708
Car Parking: Street Parking
Coach Parking: Street Parking
Nearest Railway Station: Kearsney (1 mile)
Nearest Bus Station: Pencester Road, Dover (1.5 miles)
Club Shop: Yes
Opening Times: Matchdays Only
Telephone No.: (0304) 240041
Postal Sales: Yes
Nearest Police Station: Dover
Police Force: Kent County Constabulary
Police Telephone No.: (0304) 240055

GROUND INFORMATION
Away Supporters' Entrances: No Segregation
Away Supporters' Sections: -

DISABLED SUPPORTERS INFORMATION
Wheelchairs: Accommodated
Disabled Toilets: None
The Blind: No Special Facilities

ADMISSION INFO (1993/94 PRICES)
Adult Standing: £4.50
Adult Seating: £5.50
Child Standing: £2.50
Child Seating: £3.00
Programme Price: £1.00
FAX Number: (0304) 210273

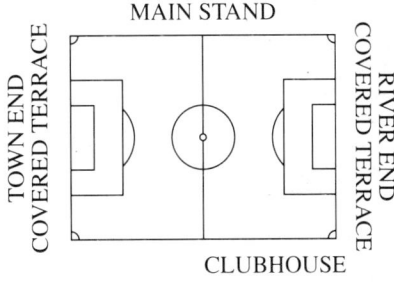

Travelling Supporters Information:
Routes: By A2 to Whitfield roundabout. Take 4th exit down hill to mini-roundabout - turn left - go 1 mile to traffic lights on hill. Turn sharp right, under railway bridge - ground is on left a further 300 yards.

GATESHEAD FC

Founded: 1930 (Reformed 1977)
Former Name(s): Gateshead United
Nickname: 'Tynesiders'
Ground: International Stadium, Neilson Road, Gateshead NE10 0EF
Record Attendance: 5,012 (20/8/84)

Colours: Shirts - White
Shorts - Black
Telephone No.: (091) 478-3883
Daytime Phone No.: (091) 478-3883
Pitch Size: 106 × 70yds
Ground Capacity: 11,500
Seating Capacity: 11,500

GENERAL INFORMATION
Supporters Club Administrator: Ian Mearns
Address: 192 Rodsley Avenue, Gateshead, Tyne & Wear
Telephone Number: (091) 490-0541
Car Parking: At Stadium
Coach Parking: At Stadium
Nearest Railway Station: Gateshead Metro (0.5 mile)
Nearest Bus Station: Gallowgate, Newcastle (2 miles)
Club Shop: Yes - At Stadium
Opening Times: Matchdays Only
Telephone No.: (091) 478-3883
Postal Sales: Yes
Nearest Police Station: Gateshead
Police Force: Northumbria
Police Telephone No.: (091) 232-3451

GROUND INFORMATION
Away Supporters' Entrances: None Specified
Away Supporters' Sections: None Specified

DISABLED SUPPORTERS INFORMATION
Wheelchairs: Wheelchair lift available in Grandstand
Disabled Toilets: Yes
The Blind: No Special Facilities

ADMISSION INFO (1993/94 PRICES)
Adult Standing: None
Adult Seating: £4.00
Child Standing: None
Child Seating: £2.00
Programme Price: 50p
FAX Number: (091) 477-1315

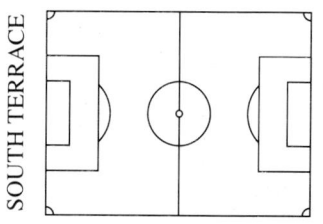

Travelling Supporters Information:
Routes: Take A1(M) to end of Motorway, then exit onto A6115 towards Gateshead. Carry on for 3 miles then carry straight on at roundabout into Park Road. Ground is on right.

HALIFAX TOWN FC

Founded: 1911
Turned Professional: 1911
Limited Company: 1911
Admitted to League: 1921
Former Name(s): None
Nickname: 'Shaymen'
Ground: Shay Ground, Shay Syke, Halifax HX1 2YS

Record Attendance: 36,885 (14/2/53)
Colours: Shirts - Blue & White
Shorts - White
Telephone No.: (0422) 353423
Daytime Phone No.: (0422) 353423
Pitch Size: 110 × 70yds
Ground Capacity: 8,049
Seating Capacity: 1,896

GENERAL INFORMATION
Supporters Club Administrator: Secretary, Stephen Kell
Address: Halifax Town Promotions, 7 Clare Road, Halifax
Telephone Number: (0422) 203360
Car Parking: Shaw Hill Car Park (Nearby)
Coach Parking: Calderdale Bus Depot (Shaw Hill)
Nearest Railway Station: Halifax (3 mins.)
Nearest Bus Station: Halifax
Club Shop:
Opening Times: Weekdays 9.30-5.00 (Except Thursdays) & Matchdays
Telephone No.: (0422) 366593
Postal Sales: Yes
Nearest Police Station: Halifax (0.25 mile)
Police Force: West Yorkshire
Police Telephone No.: (0422) 360333

GROUND INFORMATION
Away Supporters' Entrances: Shay Syke turnstiles
Away Supporters' Sections: Visitor's enclosure, Shay Syke

DISABLED SUPPORTERS INFORMATION
Wheelchairs: Accommodated in Disabled Section
Disabled Toilets: Yes
The Blind: No Special Facilities

ADMISSION INFO (1993/94 PRICES)
Adult Standing: £5.00
Adult Seating: £6.00
Child Standing: £2.00
Child Seating: £3.00
Programme Price: £1.00
FAX Number: (0422) 349487

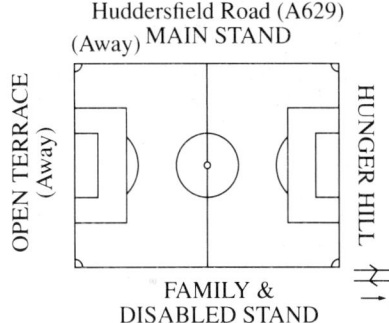

Travelling Supporters Information:
Routes: From North: Take A629 to Halifax Town Centre. Take 2nd exit at roundabout into Broad Street and follow signs for Huddersfield (A629) into Skircoat Road; From South, East & West: Exit M62 junction 24 and follow Halifax (A629) signs to Town Centre into Skircoat Road for Ground.

Kettering Town FC

Founded: 1875
Former Name(s): None
Nickname: 'The Poppies'
Ground: Rockingham Road, Kettering, Northants
Record Attendance: 11,526 (1947-48)

Colours: Shirts - Red
            Shorts - Red
Telephone No.: (0536) 83028/410815
Daytime Phone No.: (0536) 83028
Pitch Size: 110 × 70yds
Ground Capacity: 6,500
Seating Capacity: 1,800

GENERAL INFORMATION
Supporters Trust Administrator: Mr. M. Freeman
Address: -
Telephone Number: (0536) 512068
Car Parking: At Ground
Coach Parking: Cattle Market, Northfield Avenue, Kettering
Nearest Railway Station: Kettering (1 mile)
Nearest Bus Station: -
Club Shop: Yes
Opening Times: Matchdays Only
Telephone No.: (0536) 83028
Postal Sales: Yes
Nearest Police Station: London Road, Kettering
Police Force: Northants
Police Telephone No.: (0536) 411411

GROUND INFORMATION
Away Supporters' Entrances: Rockingham Road
Away Supporters' Sections: Rockingham Road End

DISABLED SUPPORTERS INFORMATION
Wheelchairs: Accommodated - in Main Stand Lower Tier East Stand
Disabled Toilets: None
The Blind: No Special Facilities

ADMISSION INFO (1993/94 PRICES)
Adult Standing: £4.00
Adult Seating: £6.00
Child Standing: £2.50
Child Seating: £3.00
Programme Price: £1.00
FAX Number: (0536) 412273

```
              BRITANNIA ROAD
         ┌─────────────────────┐
C        │                     │  R
O        │                     │  O
W        │    ○         ○      │  C
P        │                     │  K
E        │         ○           │  I
R        │                     │  N
         │    ○         ○      │  G
S        │                     │  H
T        │                     │  A
R        │                     │  M
E        │                     │
E        │                     │  R
T        │                     │  O
         │                     │  A
         │                     │  D
         └─────────────────────┘  (Away)
              MAIN STAND
```

Travelling Supporters Information:
Routes: The Ground is situated to the North of Kettering (1 mile) on the main A6003 Rockingham Road (to Oakham).

KIDDERMINSTER HARRIERS FC

Founded: 1886
Former Name(s): None
Nickname: 'Harriers'
Ground: Aggborough, Hoo Road, Kidderminster, Worcestershire
Record Attendance: 9,155 (1948)

Colours: Shirts - Red & White Halves
Shorts - Red
Telephone No.: (0562) 823931
Daytime Phone No.: (0562) 823931 or (0831) 511937
Pitch Size: 112 × 72yds
Ground Capacity: 5,600
Seating Capacity: 300

GENERAL INFORMATION
Supporters Club Administrator: R. Mercer
Address: c/o Club
Telephone Number: (0562) 823931
Car Parking: At Ground
Coach Parking: At Ground
Nearest Railway Station: Kidderminster
Nearest Bus Station: Kidderminster Town Centre
Club Shop: Yes
Opening Times: Weekdays 9.00 - 5.00 & First Team Matchdays
Telephone No.: (0562) 823931
Postal Sales: Yes
Nearest Police Station: Habberley Road, Kidderminster
Police Force: West Mercia
Police Telephone No.: (0562) 820888

GROUND INFORMATION
Away Supporters' Entrances: None Specified
Away Supporters' Sections: South Stand

DISABLED SUPPORTERS INFORMATION
Wheelchairs: Accommodated in front of Main Stand
Disabled Toilets: None
The Blind: No Special Facilities

ADMISSION INFO (1993/94 PRICES)
Adult Standing: £4.50
Adult Seating: £5.50
Child Standing: £2.50
Child Seating: £3.50
Programme Price: £1.00
FAX Number: (0562) 827329
Junior Supporters Under 14's Club-Members: £7.00 per season

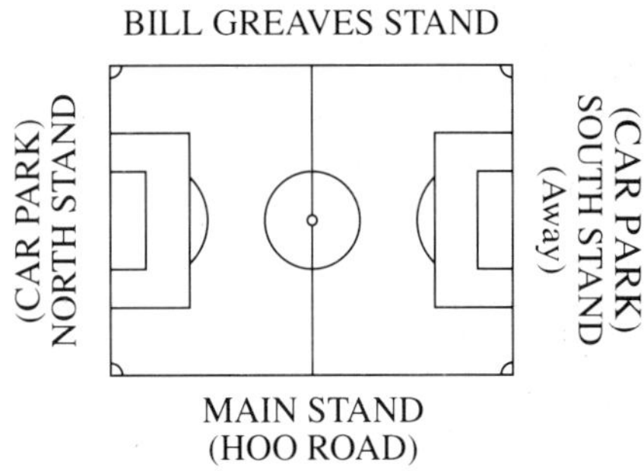

```
           BILL GREAVES STAND
         ┌─────────────────────┐
(CAR PARK)│                     │(CAR PARK)
NORTH STAND                      SOUTH STAND
         │                     │  (Away)
         └─────────────────────┘
              MAIN STAND
              (HOO ROAD)
```

Travelling Supporters Information:
Routes: From North & Midlands: Exit M5 (junction 3) on to A491 then left to A456 and follow Kidderminster signs. When in town turn left at first traffic lights and right at second traffic lights into Comberton Road. Turn left into Hoo Road at bottom of hill before ring road; From South & West: Exit M5 (junction 6) and follow signs to Kidderminster (12 miles) (A449) turn right at 1st roundabout then 1st left into Hoo Road.

MACCLESFIELD TOWN FC

Founded: 1875
Former Name(s): Macclesfield FC
Nickname: 'The Silkmen'
Ground: Moss Rose Ground, London Road, Macclesfield, Cheshire
Record Attendance: 10,041 (1948)

Colours: Shirts - Blue
Shorts - White
Telephone No.: (0625) 424324
Daytime Phone No.: (0625) 20333
Pitch Size: 110 × 72yds
Ground Capacity: 10,000
Seating Capacity: 600

GENERAL INFORMATION
Supporters Club Administrator: Carole Wood
Address: Warwick Road, Macclesfield
Telephone Number: (0625) 617670
Car Parking: Ample near Ground
Coach Parking: Near Ground
Nearest Railway Station: Macclesfield (1 mile)
Nearest Bus Station: Macclesfield
Club Shop:
Opening Times: Midweek 7.00-7.30 Matchdays 2.00-3.00
Telephone No.: (0625) 613534
Postal Sales: Yes
Nearest Police Station: Macclesfield
Police Force: Cheshire
Police Telephone No.: (0625) 610000

GROUND INFORMATION
Away Supporters' Entrances: Moss Lane
Away Supporters' Sections: Star Lane

DISABLED SUPPORTERS INFORMATION
Wheelchairs: Accommodated in front of stand
Disabled Toilets: None
The Blind: No Special Facilities

ADMISSION INFO (1993/94 PRICES)
Adult Standing: £4.00
Adult Seating: £5.00
Child Standing: £3.00
Child Seating: £4.00
Programme Price: £1.00
FAX Number: (0625) 619021

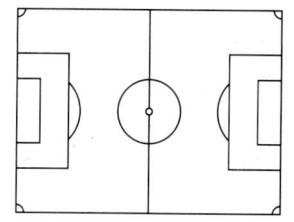

Travelling Supporters Information:
Routes: Exit M6 junction 18. Eastwards on A54, then A535 to Chelford. Turn right on to A537 to Macclesfield. Turn right from Chester Road into Crompton Road, then go left at the end along Park Lane (A536), and Park Street. Turn right into Mill Lane (A523 for Leek), then take Cross Street and London Road. Ground on left.

MERTHYR TYDFIL FC

Founded: 1945
Former Name(s): Merthyr Town FC
Nickname: 'Martyrs'
Ground: Penydarren Park, Merthyr Tydfil, Mid Glamorgan
Record Attendance: 21,000 (1949)

Colours: Shirts - White/Silver/Black Squares
Shorts - Black
Telephone No.: (0685) 371395
Daytime Phone No.: (0685) 359921
Pitch Size: 110 × 72yds
Ground Capacity: 10,000
Seating Capacity: 1,500

GENERAL INFORMATION
Supporters Club Administrator: Fred Arscott
Address: c/o Club
Telephone Number: (0685) 371395
Car Parking: Street Parking
Coach Parking: Georgetown
Nearest Railway Station: Merthyr Tydfil (0.5 mile)
Nearest Bus Station: Merthyr Tydfil
Club Shop:
Opening Times: Matchdays Only
Telephone No.: (0685) 384102
Postal Sales: Yes
Nearest Police Station: Merthyr Tydfil (0.75 mile)
Police Force: South Wales Constabulary
Police Telephone No.: (0685) 722541

GROUND INFORMATION
Away Supporters' Entrances: Theatre End
Away Supporters' Sections: Theatre End

DISABLED SUPPORTERS INFORMATION
Wheelchairs: Accommodated by Prior Arrangement
Disabled Toilets: None
The Blind: No Special Facilities

ADMISSION INFO (1993/94 PRICES)
Adult Standing: £4.00
Adult Seating: £5.00
Child Standing: £2.50
Child Seating: £3.25
Programme Price: £1.00
FAX Number: (0685) 382882
Children under 12 admitted free if with an adult.

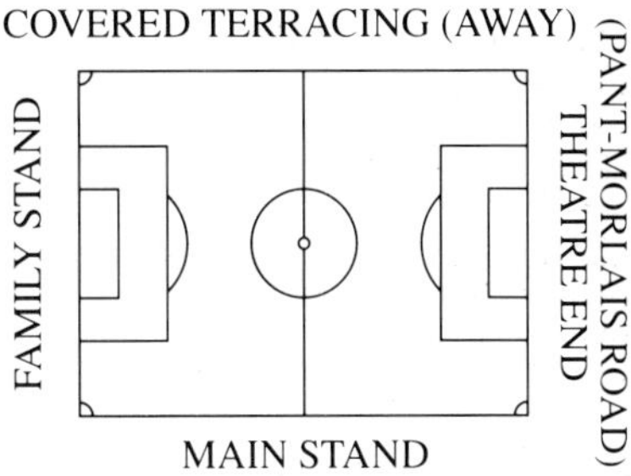

```
            COVERED TERRACING (AWAY)
                                         (PANT-MORLAIS ROAD)
         FAMILY STAND                    THEATRE END

                    MAIN STAND
```

Travelling Supporters Information:
Routes: From East: Take A465 (High Street) into Pen-y-Darren Road (about 1 mile), ground on right; From West: Take Swansea Road (A4102) past Georgetown and right into Bethesda Street, through Pant Morlais Road West into Pen-y-Darren Road. Ground on left.

NORTHWICH VICTORIA FC

Founded: 1874
Former Name(s): None
Nickname: 'The Vics'
Ground: The Drill Field, Field Road, Northwich, Cheshire
Record Attendance: 11,290 (1949)

Colours: Shirts - Green
Shorts - White
Telephone No.: (0606) 41450
Daytime Phone No.: (0606) 41450
Pitch Size: 110 × 73yds
Ground Capacity: 10,000
Seating Capacity: 660

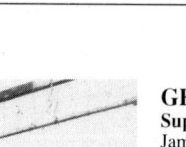

GENERAL INFORMATION
Supporters Club Administrator: James Wood
Address: c/o Club
Telephone Number: (0606) 75964
Car Parking: Street Parking
Coach Parking: Old Fire Station - adjacent
Nearest Railway Station: Northwich
Nearest Bus Station: 100 yards
Club Shop:
Opening Times: Matchdays Only
Telephone No.: (0606) 41450
Postal Sales: Yes
Nearest Police Station: Chester Way, Northwich
Police Force: Cheshire
Police Telephone No.: (0606) 48000

GROUND INFORMATION
Away Supporters' Entrances: Terminus End
Away Supporters' Sections: Terminus End

DISABLED SUPPORTERS INFORMATION
Wheelchairs: Accommodated in front of Main Stand
Disabled Toilets: None
The Blind: No Special Facilities

ADMISSION INFO (1993/94 PRICES)
Adult Standing: £4.00
Adult Seating: £5.00
Child Standing: £2.50
Child Seating: £3.50
Programme Price: £1.00
FAX Number: (0606) 330577

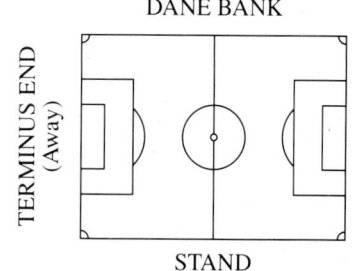

Travelling Supporters Information:
Routes: From North & South: Exit M6 junction 19 and take A556. Turn right at second roundabout (A559) and follow road for 1.5 miles - ground on right; From East & West: Take A556 to junction with A559, then as North.

RUNCORN FC

Founded: 1919
Former Name(s): None
Nickname: 'The Linnets'
Ground: Canal Street, Runcorn, Cheshire
Record Attendance: 10,111

Colours: Shirts - Yellow
Shorts - Green
Telephone No.: (0928) 560076
Daytime Phone No.: (0928) 564052
Pitch Size: 111 × 72yds
Ground Capacity: 4,735
Seating Capacity: 250 (Inc. Directors' Box)

GENERAL INFORMATION
Supporters Club Administrator: Noel Bell
Address: c/o Club
Telephone Number: (0928) 560076
Car Parking: Adjacent to Social Club
Coach Parking: Adjacent to Social Club
Nearest Railway Station: Runcorn (1 mile)
Nearest Bus Station: Runcorn Old Town (1 mile)
Club Shop: Yes
Opening Times: Matchdays Only
Telephone No.: None
Postal Sales: Yes
Nearest Police Station: Shopping City, Runcorn
Police Force: Cheshire
Police Telephone No.: (0928) 713456

GROUND INFORMATION
Away Supporters' Entrances: No routine Segregation. Some big games : - Main Stand Turnstiles 8 & 9
Away Supporters' Sections: None Specified

DISABLED SUPPORTERS INFORMATION
Wheelchairs: Not Accommodated
Disabled Toilets: None
The Blind: No Special Facilities

ADMISSION INFO (1993/94 PRICES)
Adult Standing: £4.00
Adult Seating: £5.00
Child Standing: £2.00
Child Seating: £2.50
Programme Price: 80p
FAX Number: (0928) 560076

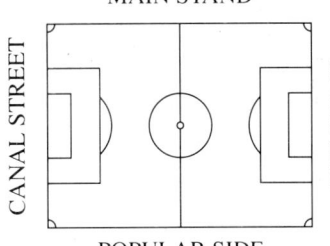

Travelling Supporters Information:
Routes: Exit M56 junction 11 and follow signs, Runcorn, Widnes, Liverpool OR Exit M62 to Widnes and cross over Runcorn & Widnes Bridge taking 2nd exit to Ground.

SLOUGH TOWN FC

Founded: 1890
Limited Company: 1991
Former Name(s): Slough, Slough United
Nickname: 'The Rebels'
Ground: Wexham Park Stadium, Wexham Road, Slough   SL2 5QR
Record Attendance: 5,000 (1982)

Colours: Shirts - Amber
      Shorts - Navy Blue
Telephone No.: (0753) 523358
Daytime Phone No.: (0753) 523358
Pitch Size: 117 × 72yds
Ground Capacity: 5,000
Seating Capacity: 395

GENERAL INFORMATION
Supporters Club Administrator: Chris Sliski
Address: 143 Knolton Way, Slough
Telephone Number: (0753) 526891
Car Parking: Car Park at Ground
Coach Parking: At Ground
Nearest Railway Station: Slough (1 mile)
Nearest Bus Station: Slough (1 mile)
Club Shop: Yes - In Clubhouse
Opening Times: Daily
Telephone No.: (0753) 523358
Postal Sales: No
Nearest Police Station: Slough
Police Force: Thames Valley
Police Telephone No.: (0753) 506000

GROUND INFORMATION
Away Supporters' Entrances: North End to right of Clubhouse (Normally No Segregation)
Away Supporters' Sections: Training Pitch End/ North End

DISABLED SUPPORTERS INFORMATION
Wheelchairs: Accommodated in front of Main Stand
Disabled Toilets: In Clubhouse
The Blind: No Special Facilities

ADMISSION INFO (1992/93 PRICES)
Adult Standing: £4.00
Adult Seating: £5.00
Child Standing: £2.00   **Programme**: £1.00
Child Seating: £2.50   **Fax**: (0753) 415956

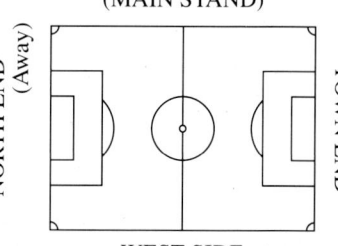

Travelling Supporters Information:
Routes: From North: Take the M25 to junction 16 and join M40. Exit at junction 1, Follow A412 (South) through Iver Heath to George Green. At the 2nd set of traffic lights turn right by the George Public House in George Green. Church Lane is 1 mile to the end, then turn left at the small roundabout and the ground is 0.25 mile on the right; From East: Take the M25 to junction 15 and join M4. Exit at junction 5 and follow A4 westbound as far as the Co-op Superstore on the right. Join A412 Northbound towards Uxbridge and follow the dual carriageway to the 4th set of traffic lights. Enter Church Lane, then as North; From South: (from Windsor Direction) Take A355 then onto the M4 and exit at junction 6 onto the A4. Turn right, pass Brunel Bus Station on left, Tesco Superstore, also on the left then turn first left into Wexham Road, signposted Wexham Park Hospital. Ground is just over 1 mile on the left; From West: Take M4 to junction 6 then follow route from South.

SOUTHPORT FC

Founded: 1881
Former Name(s): Southport Vulcan FC; Southport Central FC
Nickname: 'The Sand Grounders'
Ground: Haig Avenue, Southport, Merseyside
Record Attendance: 20,010 (1936)

Colours: Shirts - Old Gold
Shorts - Black
Telephone No.: (0704) 533422
Daytime Phone No.: (0704) 211428
Pitch Size: 115 × 78yds
Ground Capacity: 6,500
Seating Capacity: 1,880

GENERAL INFORMATION
Supporters Club Administrator: Roy Morris
Address: 'Manikata', 3 Stretton Drive, Southport
Telephone Number: (0704) 211428
Car Parking: Street Parking
Coach Parking: Adjacent to Ground
Nearest Railway Station: Southport (1.5 miles)
Nearest Bus Station: Town Centre
Club Shop: Yes
Opening Times: Matchdays 2.30pm (or 7.00pm) & also at Half-time
Telephone No.: (0704) 533422
Postal Sales: Yes
Nearest Police Station: Southport
Police Force: Merseyside
Police Telephone No.: (051) 709-6010

GROUND INFORMATION
Away Supporters' Entrances: Blowick End
Away Supporters' Sections: Blowick End Terrace

DISABLED SUPPORTERS INFORMATION
Wheelchairs: Accommodated
Disabled Toilets: Yes
The Blind: No Special Facilities

ADMISSION INFO (1993/94 PRICES)
Adult Standing: £4.00
Adult Seating: £5.00
Child Standing: £2.00
Child Seating: £2.50
Programme Price: £1.00
FAX Number: (051) 448-1982

```
         MEOLS KOP TERRACE
BLOWICK END TERRACE        SCARISBRICK
                           NEW ROAD END
            HAIG AVENUE
```

Travelling Supporters Information:
Routes: Exit M58 at junction 2 and take the A570 to Southport. At the first roundabout turn left into Scarisbrick New Road, pass over brook and turn right into Haig Avenue. Ground is on the right.

STAFFORD RANGERS FC

Founded: 1876
Former Name(s): None
Nickname: 'The Boro'
Ground: Marston Road, Stafford   ST16 3BX
Record Attendance: 8,523 (4/1/75)

Colours: Shirts - Black & White Stripes
Shorts - White
Telephone No.: (0785) 42750
Daytime Phone No.: (0785) 42750
Pitch Size: 112 × 75yds
Ground Capacity: 3,472
Seating Capacity: 426

GENERAL INFORMATION
Supporters Club Administrator: Chris Elsley
Address: 326 Sandon Road, Stafford
Telephone Number: (0785) 41954
Car Parking: At Ground
Coach Parking: Chell Road, Stafford
Nearest Railway Station: Stafford (2 miles)
Nearest Bus Station: Stafford
Club Shop: Yes
Opening Times: Matchdays Only
Telephone No.: (0785) 42750
Postal Sales: Yes
Nearest Police Station: Stafford
Police Force: Staffs
Police Telephone No.: (0785) 58151

GROUND INFORMATION
Away Supporters' Entrances: Lotus End
Away Supporters' Sections: Lotus End

DISABLED SUPPORTERS INFORMATION
Wheelchairs: Accommodated on touchline
Disabled Toilets: None
The Blind: Facilities by Arrangement

ADMISSION INFO (1993/94 PRICES)
Adult Standing: £4.00
Adult Seating: £5.00
Child Standing: £2.50
Child Seating: £3.50
Programme Price: £1.00
FAX Number: (0785) 54050

```
              LOTUS END
     ┌─────────────────────────┐
     │        │         │       │
 S   │    ┌───┤         ├───┐   │  T
 A   │    │   │    ○    │   │   │  O
 L   │    │   │         │   │   │  W
 T   │    └───┤         ├───┘   │  N
     │        │         │       │
 W   │                          │  E
 O   │                          │  N
 R   │                          │  D
 K   │                          │
 S   │                          │
     │                          │
 E   │                          │
 N   │                          │
 D   └─────────────────────────┘
          MARSTON ROAD END
```

Travelling Supporters Information:
Routes: Exit M6 junction 14 and take slip road signposted 'Stone/Stafford'. Continue to traffic island and go straight across then take 3rd right into Common Road, signposted 'Common Road/Aston Fields Industrial Estate'. Follow road to bridge and bear left over bridge, ground on right.

STALYBRIDGE CELTIC FC

Founded: 1911
Former Name(s): Stalybridge Rovers
Nickname: 'Celtic'
Ground: Bower Fold, Mottram Road, Stalybridge, Cheshire
Record Attendance: 13,500

Colours: Shirts - Blue
Shorts - Blue
Telephone No.: (061) 338-2828
Daytime Phone No.: (061) 338-2828
Pitch Size: 120 × 72yds
Ground Capacity: 4,800
Seating Capacity: 409

GENERAL INFORMATION
Supporters Club Administrator: John Hall
Address: 44 Chunal Lane, Glossop, Derbyshire
Telephone Number: (0457) 869262
Car Parking: At Ground
Coach Parking: At Ground
Nearest Railway Station: Stalybridge (1 ml)
Nearest Bus Station: Stalybridge town centre
Club Shop: Yes
Opening Times: 10.00-4.00pm every day (except Tuesdays)
Telephone No.: (061) 338-2828
Postal Sales: Yes
Nearest Police Station: Stalybridge Town Centre
Police Force: Greater Manchester
Police Telephone No.: (061) 330-8321

GROUND INFORMATION
Away Supporters' Entrances: Mottram End
Away Supporters' Sections: Mottram End

DISABLED SUPPORTERS INFORMATION
Wheelchairs: Accommodated
Disabled Toilets: Yes (rear of Main Stand)
The Blind: No Special Facilities

ADMISSION INFO (1993/94 PRICES)
Adult Standing: £4.00
Adult Seating: £5.00
Child Standing: £3.00
Child Seating: £4.00
Programme Price: £1.00
FAX Number: (061) 338-8256

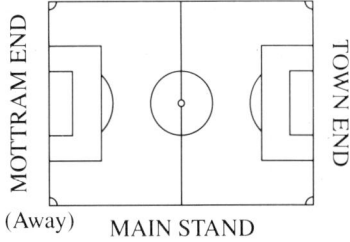

Travelling Supporters Information:
Routes: From M1 or Sheffield: Take Woodhead Pass Road to Mottram and Stalybridge; From M62: Oldham, Ashton, Stalybridge. Ground in Mottram Road near to Hare and Hounds Pub.

TELFORD UNITED FC

Founded: 1877
Former Name(s): Wellington Town FC
Nickname: 'Lillywhites'
Ground: Bucks Head Ground, Watling Street, Wellington, Telford, Shropshire
Record Attendance: 13,000 (1935)

Colours: Shirts - White
Shorts - Blue
Telephone No.: (0952) 223838
Daytime Phone No.: (0952) 292929
Pitch Size: 110 × 75yds
Ground Capacity: 10,000
Seating Capacity: 1,222

GENERAL INFORMATION
Supporters Club Administrator: The Secretary
Address: c/o Club
Telephone Number: (0952) 223838
Car Parking: At Ground
Coach Parking: At Ground
Nearest Railway Station: Wellington - Telford West
Nearest Bus Station: -
Club Shop: Yes
Opening Times: Matchdays Only
Telephone No.: (0952) 223838
Postal Sales: Yes
Nearest Police Station: Wellington
Police Force: West Mercia
Police Telephone No.: (0952) 290888

GROUND INFORMATION
Away Supporters' Entrances: North Bank Turnstiles
Away Supporters' Sections: North Bank

DISABLED SUPPORTERS INFORMATION
Wheelchairs: Accommodated in Covered Area
Disabled Toilets: None
The Blind: No Special Facilities

ADMISSION INFO (1993/94 PRICES)
Adult Standing: £4.00
Adult Seating: £6.00
Child Standing: £2.50
Child Seating: £3.50
Programme Price: £1.00
FAX Number: (0952) 249046

BLOCKLEYS STAND
NORTH BANK (Away)
WATLING STREET
WEST STAND

Travelling Supporters Information:
Routes: Exit M54 junction 6 and take A518 and B5061 to Wellington district of town. Ground is on B5061 - formerly the main A5.

WELLING UNITED FC

Founded: 1963
Former Name(s): None
Nickname: 'The Wings'
Ground: Park View Road Ground, Welling, Kent
Record Attendance: 4,020 (1989/90)

Colours: Shirts - Red with White facings
Shorts - Red
Telephone No.: (081) 301-1196
Daytime Phone No.: (081) 301-1196
Pitch Size: 112 × 72yds
Ground Capacity: 5,500
Seating Capacity: 500

GENERAL INFORMATION
Supporters Club Administrator: -
Address: c/o Club
Telephone Number: -
Car Parking: Street Parking Only
Coach Parking: Outside Ground
Nearest Railway Station: Welling (0.75 ml)
Nearest Bus Station: Bexleyheath
Club Shop: Yes
Opening Times: Matchdays Only
Telephone No.: (081) 301-1196
Postal Sales: Yes
Nearest Police Station: Welling (0.5 mile)
Police Force: Metropolitan
Police Telephone No.: (081) 304-3161

GROUND INFORMATION
Away Supporters' Entrances: -
Away Supporters' Sections: Danson Park End

DISABLED SUPPORTERS INFORMATION
Wheelchairs: Accommodated
Disabled Toilets: None
The Blind: No Special Facilities

ADMISSION INFO (1993/94 PRICES)
Adult Standing: £4.50
Adult Seating: £5.50
Child Standing: £2.50
Child Seating: £3.50
Programme Price: £1.00
FAX Number: (081) 301-5676

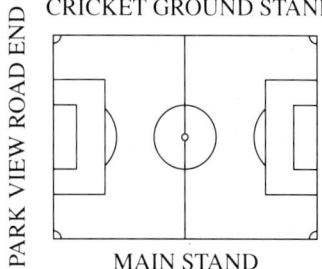

Travelling Supporters Information:
Routes: Take A2 (Rochester Way) from London, then A221 Northwards (Danson Road) to Bexleyheath. At end turn left towards Welling along Park View Road. Ground on left.

WITTON ALBION FC

Founded: 1890
Turned Professional: 1908
Former Name(s): -
Nickname: 'Albion'
Ground: Wincham Park, Chapel Street, Wincham, Northwich CW9 6DA
Record Attendance: 3,800

Colours: Shirts - Red & White Stripes
Shorts - Black
Telephone No.: (0606) 43008
Daytime Phone No.: (0606) 43008
Pitch Size: 115 × 75yds
Ground Capacity: 5,000
Seating Capacity: 640

GENERAL INFORMATION
Social Club Administrator: Brian Gittings
Address: Wincham Park Social Club, Northwich CW9 6DA
Telephone Number: (0606) 47117
Car Parking: 1,200 spaces at Ground
Coach Parking: At Ground
Nearest Railway Station: Northwich
Nearest Bus Station: Northwich
Club Shop: Yes
Opening Times: Matchdays Only
Telephone No.: (0606) 43008
Postal Sales: Yes
Nearest Police Station: Northwich
Police Force: Cheshire
Police Telephone No.: (0606) 43541

GROUND INFORMATION
Away Supporters' Entrances: Lostock End
Away Supporters' Sections: Lostock End

DISABLED SUPPORTERS INFORMATION
Wheelchairs: Accommodated
Disabled Toilets: Yes
The Blind: No Information

ADMISSION INFO (1993/94 PRICES)
Adult Standing: £4.00
Adult Seating: £5.00
Child Standing: £2.50
Child Seating: £3.50
Programme Price: £1.00
FAX Number: (0606) 43008

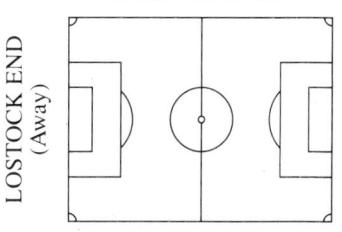

Travelling Supporters Information:
Routes: Exit M6 junction 19 and take A556 towards Northwich. After 3 miles turn right onto A559 following Warrington signs. Turn left opposite Black Greyhound Inn and ground is on left.
Alternative Route: Exit M56 junction 10 and take A559 to Black Greyhound Inn and turn right.

WOKING FC

Founded: 1889
Former Name(s): None
Nickname: 'Cardinals'
Ground: Kingfield Sports Ground, Kingsfield Road, Woking, Surrey GU22 9AA
Record Attendance: 6,000

Colours: Shirts - Red
            Shorts - White
Telephone No.: (0483) 772470
Daytime Phone No.: (0483) 757588
Pitch Size: 113 × 70yds
Ground Capacity: 6,000
Seating Capacity: 500

GENERAL INFORMATION
Supporters Club Administrator: K. Raymond
Address: c/o Club
Telephone Number: (0483) 772470
Car Parking: 150 cars at Ground
Coach Parking: At Ground
Nearest Railway Station: Woking (1 mile)
Nearest Bus Station: Woking
Club Shop: Yes
Opening Times: All Week & Matchdays
Telephone No.: (0483) 776126/772470
Postal Sales: Yes
Nearest Police Station: Woking
Police Force: Surrey
Police Telephone No.: (0483) 761991

GROUND INFORMATION
Away Supporters' Entrances: Kingfield Road or Westfield Avenue (if segregation in force)
Away Supporters' Sections: Arranged if Required

DISABLED SUPPORTERS INFORMATION
Wheelchairs: Accommodated, Please contact club for details
Disabled Toilets: Yes
The Blind: No Special Facilities

ADMISSION INFO (1993/94 PRICES)
Adult Standing: £4.50
Adult Seating: £5.70
Child Standing: £2.80
Child Seating: £4.00
Programme Price: £1.00
FAX Number: (0483) 776126

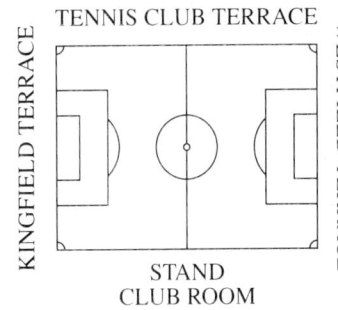

Travelling Supporters Information:
Routes: Exit M25 junction 10 and follow A30 towards Guildford, leave at next junction on B2215 through Ripley to join A247 to Woking OR Exit M25 junction 11 and follow A320 to Woking Town Centre, Ground on outskirts - follow signs on A320 then A247.

YEOVIL TOWN FC

Founded: 1923
Former Name(s): Yeovil & Petters United FC
Nickname: 'Glovers'
Ground: Huish Park, Lufton Way, Yeovil, Somerset BA22 8YF
Record Attendance: 8,618

Colours: Shirts - Green & White Stripes
            Shorts - White
Telephone No.: (0935) 23662
Daytime Phone No.: (0935) 23662
Pitch Size: 115 × 72yds
Ground Capacity: 8,720
Seating Capacity: 5,212

GENERAL INFORMATION
Supporters Club Administrator: -
Address: c/o Club
Telephone Number: -
Car Parking: Car Parks for (750/1000 cars)
Coach Parking: At Ground
Nearest Railway Station: Yeovil Pen Mill (2.5 miles); Yeovil Junction (3.5 miles)
Nearest Bus Station: Yeovil (2 miles)
Club Shop: Yes
Opening Times: Monday to Friday 9.30-4.30 & Matchdays
Telephone No.: (0935) 23662
Postal Sales: Yes
Nearest Police Station: Yeovil
Police Force: Avon & Somerset
Police Telephone No.: (0935) 75291

GROUND INFORMATION
Away Supporters' Entrances: Copse Road
Away Supporters' Sections: Visitors End

DISABLED SUPPORTERS INFORMATION
Wheelchairs: Accommodated - in Bartlett Stand
Disabled Toilets: Yes
The Blind: No Special Facilities

ADMISSION INFO (1993/94 PRICES)
Adult Standing: £4.20
Adult Seating: £4.50 - £5.00
Child Standing: £2.30
Child Seating: £2.50 - £3.20
(Family Tickets are available at discounted rates)
Programme Price: £1.00
FAX Number: (0935) 73956

```
            BARTLETT STAND
        ┌─────────────────────┐
   V    │                     │   H
   I    │                     │   O
   S    │                     │   M
   I    │         ○           │   E
   T    │                     │
   O    │                     │   E
   R    │                     │   N
   S    │                     │   D
        │                     │
   E    │                     │
   N    │                     │
   D    └─────────────────────┘
              MAIN STAND
```

Travelling Supporters Information:
Routes: From London: Take M3 and A303 to Cartgate Roundabout. Enter Yeovil on A3088. Take 1st exit at next roundabout & straight across next roundabout into Western Avenue, turn left into Copse Road, where spectator parking is sited; From North: Exit M5 junction 25 and take A358 (Ilminster) and A303 (Eastbound) entering Yeovil on A3088, then follow directions as London.

AYLESBURY UNITED FC

Founded: 1897
Former Name(s): None
Nickname: 'The Ducks'
Ground: The Stadium, Buckingham Road, Aylesbury, Bucks
Record Attendance: 6,031

Colours: Shirts - Green & White
Shorts - Green
Telephone No.: (0296) 436350
Daytime Phone No.: (0296) 436350
Pitch Size: 112 × 74yds
Ground Capacity: 4,035
Seating Capacity: 400

GENERAL INFORMATION
Supporters Club Administrator: Mike Quinn
Address: c/o Club
Telephone Number: (0296) 436350
Car Parking: 250 Cars at Ground
Coach Parking: At Ground
Nearest Railway Station: Aylesbury Town (20 minutes walk)
Nearest Bus Station: Aylesbury Bus Station (20 minutes walk)
Club Shop: At Ground
Opening Times: Matchdays & Office Hours
Telephone No.: (0296) 436350
Postal Sales: Yes
Nearest Police Station: Aylesbury
Police Force: Thames Valley
Police Telephone No.: (0296) 396000

GROUND INFORMATION
Away Supporters' Entrances: Country End
Away Supporters' Sections: Country End

DISABLED SUPPORTERS INFORMATION
Wheelchairs: Accommodated in Main Stand
Disabled Toilets: In Clubhouse
The Blind: Not Special Facilities

ADMISSION INFO (1993/94 PRICES)
Adult Standing: £4.00
Adult Seating: £5.00
Child Standing: £2.00
Child Seating: £2.50
Programme Price: £1.00
FAX Number: (0296) 395667

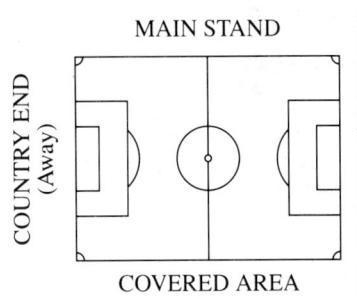

Travelling Supporters Information:
Routes: From Buckingham Direction: On outskirts of town, on left; From all other directions: follow signs A413 Buckingham, ground on outskirts of town on right.

BASINGSTOKE TOWN FC

Founded: 1896
Former Name(s): None
Nickname: 'Stoke'
Ground: Camrose Ground, Western Way, Basingstoke, Hants
Record Attendance: 4,023 vs Torquay United (1989)

Colours: Shirts - Blue with Gold Trim
Shorts - Blue with Gold Trim
Telephone No.: (0256) 461465/464353
Daytime Phone No.: (0734) 597700
Pitch Size: 110 × 70yds
Ground Capacity: 5,000
Seating Capacity: 750

photo: Sean Dillow - Basingstoke Gazette

GENERAL INFORMATION
Supporters Club Administrator: R.Lockyer
Address: c/o Camrose Ground, Western Way, Basingstoke, Hants.
Telephone Number: (0256) 461465
Car Parking: 600 Cars at Ground
Coach Parking: Ample room provided
Nearest Railway Station: Basingstoke
Nearest Bus Station: Basingstoke Town Centre (2 miles)
Club Shop: Yes
Opening Times: Matchdays one hour before kick-off and during game
Telephone No.: (0256) 461465
Postal Sales: Yes
Nearest Police Station: Basingstoke Town Centre
Police Force: Hampshire
Police Telephone No.: (0256) 473111

GROUND INFORMATION
Away Supporters' Entrances: No usual segregation
Away Supporters' Sections: -

DISABLED SUPPORTERS INFORMATION
Wheelchairs: Area available for wheelchairs
Disabled Toilets: None
The Blind: No Special Facilities

ADMISSION INFO (1993/94 PRICES)
Adult Standing: £3.50
Adult Seating: £4.00
Child Standing: £2.00
Child Seating: £2.50
Programme Price: 70p
FAX Number: None

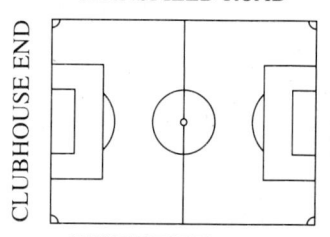

Travelling Supporters Information:
Routes: Exit M3 at junction 6, take first left at the Black Dam roundabout. At the next roundabout take the 2nd exit, then the 1st exit at the following roundabout and the 5th exit at the final roundabout. This takes you into Western Way, the ground is 50 yards on the right.

BROMLEY FC

Founded: 1892
Former Name(s): None
Nickname: 'Lilywhites'
Ground: Hayes Lane, Bromley, Kent
Record Attendance: 12,000 (24/9/49)

Colours: Shirts - White
   Shorts - Black
Telephone No.: (081) 460-9013
Daytime Phone No.: (081) 467-8837
Pitch Size: 112 × 78yds
Ground Capacity: 8,500
Seating Capacity: 2,000

GENERAL INFORMATION
Supporters Club Administrator: Jack Freeman
Address: c/o Club
Telephone Number: (081) 460-5291
Car Parking: 300 Cars at Ground
Coach Parking: At Ground
Nearest Railway Station: Bromley South (1 mile)
Nearest Bus Station: High Street, Bromley
Club Shop: Yes
Opening Times: Matchdays Only
Telephone No.: (081) 857-3961
Postal Sales: Yes
Nearest Police Station: Widmore Road, Bromley
Police Force: Metropolitan 'P' Division (3 miles)
Police Telephone No.: (081) 697-9212

GROUND INFORMATION
Away Supporters' Entrances: No Segregation
Away Supporters' Sections: No Segregation

DISABLED SUPPORTERS INFORMATION
Wheelchairs: Accommodated
Disabled Toilets: None
The Blind: No Special Facilities

ADMISSION INFO (1993/94 PRICES)
Adult Standing: £3.00
Adult Seating: £3.00
Child Standing: £1.50
Child Seating: £1.50
Programme Price: 60p
FAX Number: -

NOTE: Due to a serious fire, the ground is not in use at present, but should be re-opened later in the 1993/94 season.

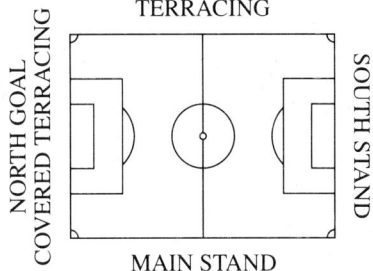

Travelling Supporters Information:
Routes: Exit M25 at A21 turnoff for Bromley and follow to A232 Croydon to Orpington Road. 1.5 miles past West Wickham (on Hayes Common), turn left into Baston Road (B265). Follow along into Hayes Street and then Hayes Lane. Ground is 0.5 mile along Hayes Lane on the right, set back from the road.

CARSHALTON ATHLETIC FC

Founded: 1905
Former Name(s): None
Nickname: 'The Robins'
Ground: War Memorial Sports Ground, Colston Avenue, Carshalton, Surrey
Record Attendance: 7,800

Colours: Shirts - Maroon with White Trim
Shorts - White
Telephone No.: (081) 770-3601
Daytime Phone No.: (081) 764-6233
Pitch Size: 117 × 76yds
Ground Capacity: 8,000
Seating Capacity: 240

GENERAL INFORMATION
Supporters Club Administrator: Sylvia Collier
Address: c/o Club
Telephone Number: (081) 715-2229
Car Parking: Space for 80 Cars at Ground
Coach Parking: At Ground
Nearest Railway Station: Carshalton (200 yards)
Nearest Bus Station: 400 yards
Club Shop: Yes
Opening Times: Matchdays Only
Telephone No.: -
Postal Sales: Yes
Nearest Police Station: Sutton
Police Force: Metropolitan
Police Telephone No.: (081) 680-6212

GROUND INFORMATION
Away Supporters' Entrances: No Segregation
Away Supporters' Sections: -

DISABLED SUPPORTERS INFORMATION
Wheelchairs: Not Accommodated
Disabled Toilets: None
The Blind: No Special Facilities

ADMISSION INFO (1993/94 PRICES)
Adult Standing: £3.50
Adult Seating: £4.00
Child Standing: £1.50
Child Seating: £2.00
Programme Price: 60p
FAX Number: -

```
                COVERED TERRACE
                  (PARK SIDE)
         ┌─────────────────────────┐  C C
         │                         │  A O
         │                         │  R V
    F    │                         │     E
    L    │                         │  P R
    A    │                         │  A E
    T    │                         │  R D
         │                         │  K
    T    │                         │     T
    E    │                         │  &  E
    R    │                         │     R
    R    │                         │  T  R
    A    │                         │  U  A
    C    │                         │  R  C
    E    │                         │  N  E
         │                         │  S
         └─────────────────────────┘  T
                 MAIN STAND           I
                                      L
                                      E
                                      S
```

Travelling Supporters Information:
Routes: From London: Pick up the A23 at The Elephant & Castle or The Oval. Continue along The Brixton Road (A23), through Brixton up Brixton Hill and continue past Streatham Hill to Streatham High Road (still on the A23). At the traffic lights on the junction at St.Leonard's Church, cross into Mitcham Lane (A216), continue through Streatham Road and bear left at the traffic lights at Figgs Marsh onto London Road (A217) and follow A217 through Bishopsford Road until reaching the Rose Hill roundabout. At roundabout take 1st exit into Wrythe Lane and continue for 1 mile, then turn right into Colston Avenue just before railway bridge. Ground 150 yards on right. A Private road leads to the Stadium and Car park; From the M25: Exit junction 8 on to A217 passing Lower Kingswood, Kingswood Burgh Heath, Banstead until roundabout before sign to Sutton. Bear left, still on the A217 until the Rose Hill roundabout is reached, take 4th exit then as above.

CHESHAM UNITED FC

Founded: 1887
Former Name(s): Chesham Generals FC & Chesham Town FC
Nickname: 'The Generals'
Ground: Meadow Park, Amy Lane, Chesham, Bucks
Record Attendance: 5,000 (5/12/79)

Colours: Shirts - Claret & Blue
Shorts - Claret & Blue
Telephone No.: (0494) 783964
Daytime Phone No.: (0494) 783964
Pitch Size: 120 × 80yds
Ground Capacity: 5,000
Seating Capacity: 250

GENERAL INFORMATION
Supporters Club Administrator: Brian Cooper
Address: c/o Club
Telephone Number: (0494) 784072
Car Parking: At Ground
Coach Parking: At Ground
Nearest Railway Station: Chesham (0.5 ml)
Nearest Tube Station: Chesham (10 mins)
Club Shop: Yes
Opening Times: Matchdays Only
Telephone No.: -
Postal Sales: Yes
Nearest Police Station: Chesham Broad Street, Chesham
Police Force: Thames Valley
Police Telephone No.: (0494) 431133

GROUND INFORMATION
Away Supporters' Entrances: None Specified
Away Supporters' Sections: None Specified

DISABLED SUPPORTERS INFORMATION
Wheelchairs: No Special Facilities
Disabled Toilets: None
The Blind: No Special Facilities

ADMISSION INFO (1993/94 PRICES)
Adult Standing: £4.00
Adult Seating: £5.00
Child Standing: £2.00   (Children under 12 - free)
Child Seating: £3.00   (as above)
Programme Price: £1.00
FAX Number: (0494) 791608

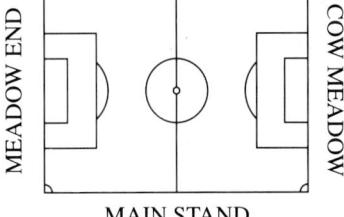

Travelling Supporters Information:
Routes: From Amersham: Take A416 to Chesham. Very sharp left at roundabout at foot of Amersham Road, into Meadow Park; From M25: Exit junction 18. Take A404 to Amersham then as above; From M40: From West, exit junction 4 and take A404 to Amersham then as above. Alternatively exit junction 2 and take A355 to Amersham then as above.

DORKING FC

Founded: 1880
Former Name(s): Guildford Dorking United FC & Dorking Town FC
Nickname: 'The Chicks'
Ground: Meadowbank, Mill Lane, Dorking, Surrey RH4 1DX
Record Attendance: 4,500 vs Folkestone (1954/55)

Colours: Shirts - Green & White Hoops Shorts - White
Telephone No.: (0306) 884112
Daytime Phone No.: (0293) 821380
Pitch Size: 110 × 72yds
Ground Capacity: 3,600
Seating Capacity: 200

GENERAL INFORMATION
Supporters Club Administrator: Brian Savory
Address: 22 Deepfield Way, Coulsdon, Surrey CR5 2SZ
Telephone Number: (081) 668-1810
Car Parking: Car Park - Nearby
Coach Parking: At Ground
Nearest Railway Station: Deepdene or Dorking (1.5 miles)
Club Shop: Yes
Opening Times: Matchdays Only
Telephone No.: (081) 668-1810
Postal Sales: Yes
Nearest Police Station: Dorking
Police Force: Metropolitan
Police Telephone No.: -

GROUND INFORMATION
Away Supporters' Entrances: No Segregation
Away Supporters' Sections: No Segregation

DISABLED SUPPORTERS INFORMATION
Wheelchairs: Accommodated
Disabled Toilets: None at present
The Blind: No Special Facilities

ADMISSION INFO (1993/94 PRICES)
Adult Standing: £3.50
Adult Seating: £4.00
Child Standing: £1.75
Child Seating: £2.00
Programme Price: 80p
FAX Number: None

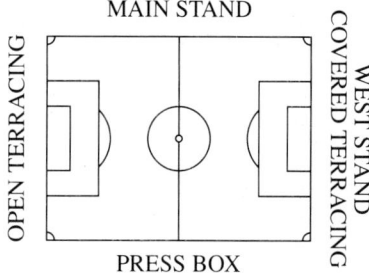

Travelling Supporters Information:
Routes: Take A25 into Dorking from Reigate or A24 from London/Worthing. At the roundabout where they meet take the A25 into the town centre (Dorking High Street). Turn right opposite White Horse Hotel and ground is on the left.

DULWICH HAMLET FC

Founded: 1893
Former Name(s): None
Nickname: 'The Hamlet'
Ground: Champion Hill Stadium, Dog Kennel Hill, London SE22 8BD
Record Attendance: 20,744 (1933)

Colours: Shirts - Pink & Blue Stripes
Shorts - Blue
Telephone No.: (071) 274-8707
Daytime Phone No.: (071) 274-8707
Pitch Size: 110 × 70yds
Ground Capacity: 3,000
Seating Capacity: 500

GENERAL INFORMATION
Supporters Club Administrator: Colin Campbell
Address: c/o Club
Telephone Number: (071) 639-6355
Car Parking: Space for 50 cars at ground
Coach Parking: At Ground
Nearest Railway Station: East Dulwich (adjacent)
Club Shop: None
Opening Times: -
Telephone No.: -
Postal Sales: -
Nearest Police Station: East Dulwich
Police Force: Metropolitan
Police Telephone No.: (081) 693-3366

GROUND INFORMATION
Away Supporters' Entrances: No Segregation
Away Supporters' Sections: No Segregation

DISABLED SUPPORTERS INFORMATION
Wheelchairs: Accommodated
Disabled Toilets: Yes
The Blind: No Special Facilities

ADMISSION INFO (1993/94 PRICES)
Adult Standing: £3.50
Adult Seating: £3.50
Child Standing: £1.75
Child Seating: £1.75
Programme Price: 60p
FAX Number: -

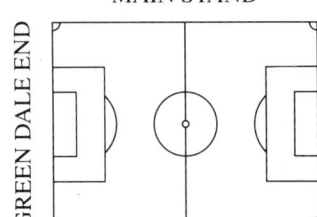

Travelling Supporters Information:
Routes: From Elephant & Castle go down Walworth Road, through Camberwell's one-way system and along Denmark Hill. Turn left by the railway into Champion Park and then right at the end down Grave Lane to the ground in Dog Kennel Hill; From the South: Come up through Streatham on the A23, turn right to Tulse Hill along the A205 (Christchurch Road) and carry on towards Sydenham. Turn left at The Grove into Lordship Lane and carry on to East Dulwich.

ENFIELD FC

Founded: 1893
Former Name(s): Enfield Spartans
Nickname: -
Ground: The Stadium, Southbury Road, Enfield, Middlesex EN1 1YQ
Record Attendance: 10,000 (10/10/62)
Colours: Shirts - White & Blue
           Shorts - White
Telephone No.: (081) 292-0665
Daytime Phone No.: (081) 292-0665
Pitch Size: 118 × 74yds
Ground Capacity: 8,500
Seating Capacity: 675

GENERAL INFORMATION
Supporters Club Administrator: Glyn Smith
Address: 71 Lincoln Way, Enfield, Middlesex EN1 1TD
Telephone Number: (081) 804-1402
Car Parking: Adjacent to Ground
Coach Parking: Adjacent to Ground
Nearest Railway Station: Enfield Town & Southbury (both 800 yards)
Nearest Bus Station: Ponders End
Club Shop: Yes
Opening Times: Matchdays Only
Telephone No.: (081) 292-0665
Postal Sales: Yes
Nearest Police Station: Enfield Town
Police Force: Metropolitan
Police Telephone No.: (081) 367-2222

GROUND INFORMATION
Away Supporters' Entrances: Cambridge Road End (Only when segregated)
Away Supporters' Sections: Cambridge Road End

DISABLED SUPPORTERS INFORMATION
Wheelchairs: Accommodated
Disabled Toilets: None
The Blind: Commentaries Available by Arrangement

ADMISSION INFO (1993/94 PRICES)
Adult Standing: £3.50
Adult Seating: £4.00
Child Standing: £2.50
Child Seating: £4.00
Programme Price: £1.00
FAX Number: (081) 292-0669

Travelling Supporters Information:
Routes: From North: Take M1 onto M25. Exit junction 25 onto A10 into Enfield; From South: Take A406 (North Circular) onto A10. Ground located at junction of A10 and A110.

GRAYS ATHLETIC FC

Founded: 1890
Former Name(s): None
Nickname: 'The Blues'
Ground: Recreation Ground, Bridge Road, Grays, Essex   RM17 6BZ
Record Attendance: 9,500 (1959)
Colours: Shirts - Blue & White
Shorts - Blue & White
Telephone No.: (0375) 377753 (Club)
Daytime Phone No.: (0375) 391649
Pitch Size: 100 × 75yds
Ground Capacity: 5,500
Seating Capacity: 350

GENERAL INFORMATION
Supporters Club Administrator: Bill Grove
Address: 141 Clarence Road, Grays, Essex   RM17 6RD
Telephone Number: (0375) 391649
Car Parking: Car Parks close to Ground
Coach Parking: Car Parks close to Ground
Nearest Railway Station: Grays
Nearest Bus Station: Grays
Club Shop: Yes
Opening Times: Matchdays Only
Telephone No.: (0375) 377753
Postal Sales: Yes
Nearest Police Station: Grays
Police Force: Essex County Constabulary
Police Telephone No.: (0375) 391212

GROUND INFORMATION
Away Supporters' Entrances: No Segregation
Away Supporters' Sections: No Segregation

DISABLED SUPPORTERS INFORMATION
Wheelchairs: Accommodated
Disabled Toilets: None
The Blind: No Special Facilities

ADMISSION INFO (1993/94 PRICES)
Adult Standing: £3.50
Adult Seating: £3.50
Child Standing: £2.00
Child Seating: £2.00
Programme Price: 60p
FAX Number: None

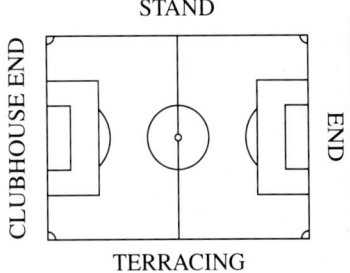

Travelling Supporters Information:
Routes: Exit M25 junctions 30-31 and take A1304. Proceed around 3 roundabouts then take 2nd right. Go straight on until Bridge Road, the Ground is on the right hand side.

HARROW BOROUGH FC

Founded: 1933
Former Name(s): Roxonians FC, Harrow Town FC
Nickname: 'The Boro'
Ground: Earlsmead, Carlyon Avenue, South Harrow, Middlesex HA2 8SS
Record Attendance: 3,000 (1946)

Colours: Shirts - Red with White Trim
Shorts - White
Telephone No.: (081) 422-5221 (Office)
Daytime Phone No.: (081) 422-5221
Pitch Size: 113 × 74yds
Ground Capacity: 3,000
Seating Capacity: 200

GENERAL INFORMATION
Supporters Club Administrator: R. Snook
Address: c/o Club
Telephone Number: (081) 422-5221
Car Parking: 90 Cars at Ground
Coach Parking: At Ground
Nearest Railway Station: Northolt Park (0.5 mile)
Nearest Tube Station: South Harrow LRT
Club Shop: Yes
Opening Times: Matchdays Only
Telephone No.: (081) 422-5221
Postal Sales: via Club
Nearest Police Station: South Harrow
Police Force: Metropolitan
Police Telephone No.: (081) 900-7212

GROUND INFORMATION
Away Supporters' Entrances: Earlsmead
Away Supporters' Sections: Earlsmead

DISABLED SUPPORTERS INFORMATION
Wheelchairs: Accommodated
Disabled Toilets: None
The Blind: No Special Facilities

ADMISSION INFO (1993/94 PRICES)
Adult Standing: £3.50
Adult Seating: £4.10
Child Standing: £2.00
Child Seating: £2.60
Programme Price: 80p
FAX Number: (081) 422-5221

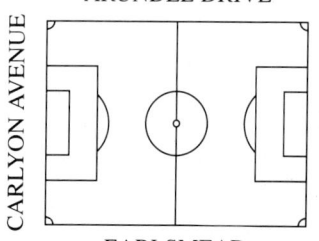

Travelling Supporters Information:
Routes: Exit M25 to M40 East, carry on to A40. Turn off at the Target PH Northolt and travel past Northolt LRT station to Traffic Lights. Turn left to roundabout (near Eastcote Arms) then right into Eastcote Lane and right into Carlyon Avenue then finally right again into Earlsmead.

HAYES FC

Founded: 1909
Former Name(s): Botwell Mission
Nickname: 'The Missioners'
Ground: Church Road, Hayes, Middlesex
Record Attendance: 15,370 (10/2/51)
Colours: Shirts - Red & White Stripes
Shorts - Black
Telephone No.: (081) 573-1932
Daytime Phone No.: (081) 573-1932
Pitch Size: 117 × 70yds
Ground Capacity: 9,500
Seating Capacity: 450

GENERAL INFORMATION
Supporters Club Administrator: Lee Hermitage
Address: c/o Hayes FC, Church Road
Telephone Number: (081) 573-4598
Car Parking: 300 Cars at Ground
Coach Parking: By arrangement
Nearest Railway Station: Hayes & Harlington (1 mile)
Nearest Bus Station: Hayes
Club Shop: Yes
Opening Times: 2.00 - 5.00pm Saturday matches; 6.45 - 9.30pm Midweek matches
Telephone No.: None
Postal Sales: Address to Lee Hermitage c/o Hayes FC
Nearest Police Station: Hayes End (Morgans Lane)
Police Force: Metropolitan
Police Telephone No.: (081) 900-7212

GROUND INFORMATION
Away Supporters' Entrances: No Segregation Usual
Away Supporters' Sections: but may be segregated at Church Road End.

DISABLED SUPPORTERS INFORMATION
Wheelchairs: Accommodated
Disabled Toilets: None
The Blind: Facilities available by arrangement

ADMISSION INFO (1993/94 PRICES)
Adult Standing: £3.50
Adult Seating: £4.00
Child Standing: £2.00
Child Seating: £2.50
Programme Price: 80p
FAX Number: (081) 756-1669

```
          COVERED STANDING
    ┌─────────────────────────┐
U   │                         │  C  C
N   │                         │  A  H
C   │                         │  R  U
O   │                         │     R
V   │                         │  P  C
E   │                         │  A  H
R   │                         │  R
E   │                         │  K  R
D   │                         │     O
    │                         │     A
    └─────────────────────────┘     D
             GRANDSTAND
```

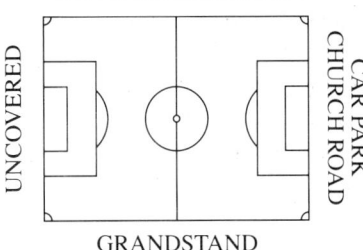

Travelling Supporters Information:
Routes: From A40: Approaching London, take Ruislip junction - turn right onto B455 Ruislip Road to White Hart Roundabout. Take Hayes by-pass to Uxbridge Road (A4020), turn right, then Church Road is 0.75 mile on the left, opposite Adam & Eve Pub. From M4: Exit junction 3 and take A312 to Parkway towards Southall, then Hayes by-pass to Uxbridge Road (A4020). Turn left, then as above.

HENDON FC

Founded: 1908
Former Name(s): Hampstead Town (1908-33); Golders Green FC (1933-46)
Nickname: 'Dons' 'Greens'
Ground: Claremont Road, Cricklewood, London NW2 1AE
Record Attendance: 9,000 (1952)

Colours: Shirts - Green
Shorts - White
Telephone No.: (081) 201-9494
Daytime Phone No.: (081) 201-9494
Pitch Size: 109 × 79yds
Ground Capacity: 8,000
Seating Capacity: 500

GENERAL INFORMATION
Supporters Club Administrator: Len Burt
Address: 140 Iverson Road, London NW6 2HL
Telephone Number: (071) 624-7017
Car Parking: Space for 200 Cars at Ground
Coach Parking: At Ground
Nearest Railway Station: Cricklewood (0.5 mile)
Nearest Tube Station: Brent Cross (0.5 mile)
Club Shop: Yes
Opening Times: Matchdays Only
Telephone No.: -
Postal Sales: Yes
Nearest Police Station: Golders Green
Police Force: Metropolitan
Police Telephone No.: (081) 200-2212

GROUND INFORMATION
Away Supporters' Entrances: No Segregation
Away Supporters' Sections: -

DISABLED SUPPORTERS INFORMATION
Wheelchairs: Not Accommodated
Disabled Toilets: None
The Blind: No Special Facilities

ADMISSION INFO (1993/94 PRICES)
Adult Standing: £4.00
Adult Seating: £5.00
Child Standing: £2.00
Child Seating: £3.00
Programme Price: 80p
FAX Number: (081) 905-5966

```
              COVERED TERRACING
         ┌─────────────────────────┐
    O    │                         │   O  C
    P    │                         │   P  A
    E    │                         │   E  R
    N    │                         │   N
         │                         │      P
    T    │                         │   T  A
    E    │                         │   E  R
    R    │                         │   R  K
    R    │                         │   R
    A    │                         │   A
    C    │                         │   C
    E    │                         │   E
         └─────────────────────────┘
                 MAIN STAND
               CLAREMONT ROAD
```

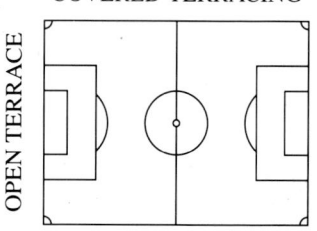

Travelling Supporters Information:
Routes: Take the M1 or North Circular Road to the southern end of the M1. At this intersection take the exit running parallel to the A406 on its eastern side (Tilling Road). Then take 2nd right into Claremont Road and ground is on right.

HITCHIN TOWN FC

Founded: 1865
Former Name(s): Hitchin Blue Cross FC
Nickname: 'The Canaries'
Ground: Top Field, Fishponds Road, Hitchin, Herts SG5 1NU
Record Attendance: 7,878 vs Wycombe Wanderers (1956)

Colours: Shirts - Yellow
Shorts - Green
Telephone No.: (0462) 434483
Daytime Phone No.: (0462) 456003
Pitch Size: 114 × 78yds
Ground Capacity: 4,000
Seating Capacity: 400

GENERAL INFORMATION
Supporters Club Administrator: Keith Farr
Address: 25 Earl Close, Eaton Socen, St.Neots, Cambs. PE19 3JW
Telephone Number: (071) 639-6355
Car Parking: Space for 150 cars at ground
Coach Parking: At Ground
Nearest Railway Station: Hitchin (1 mile)
Nearest Bus Station: Hitchin-Bancroft Terminus (0.5 mile)
Club Shop: Yes
Opening Times: Matchdays Only
Phone No.: (081) 883-2188 (Irvin Morgan)
Postal Sales: Yes
Nearest Police Station: Hitchin
Police Force: Hertfordshire
Police Telephone No.: (0438) 312323

GROUND INFORMATION
Away Supporters' Entrances: No Segregation
Away Supporters' Sections: No Segregation

DISABLED SUPPORTERS INFORMATION
Wheelchairs: Accommodated
Disabled Toilets: Yes
The Blind: No Special Facilities

ADMISSION INFO (1993/94 PRICES)
Adult Standing: £3.50
Adult Seating: £4.00
Child Standing: £2.00
Child Seating: £2.50
Programme Price: 80p
FAX Number: c/o (071) 287-8156

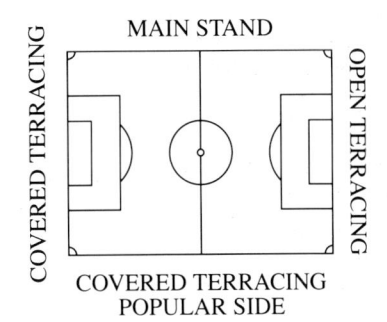

MAIN STAND
COVERED TERRACING
OPEN TERRACING
COVERED TERRACING
POPULAR SIDE

Travelling Supporters Information:
Routes: Take A1(M) to Junction 8 with A602 just north of Stevenage and follow signs for Hitchin. Upon reaching Hitchin follow A600 Bedford signs at roundabout onto southern bypass and ground is about 1.5 miles at junction of A600 and A505 - clearly visible.

KINGSTONIAN FC

Founded: 1885
Former Name(s): Kingston & Surbiton YMCA (1885-87); Saxons (1887-90); Kingston Wanderers (1890-93); Kingston on Thames (1893-1908); Old Kingstonians until 1919
Nickname: 'The K's'
Ground: Kingsmeadow Stadium, Kingston Road, Kingston upon Thames, Surrey KT1 3PB

Record Attendance: Unknown (5/2/55)
Colours: Shirts - Red & White
Shorts - Black
Telephone No.: (081) 547-3335
Daytime Phone No.: (081) 547-3335
Pitch Size: 115 × 80yds
Ground Capacity: 7,000
Seating Capacity: 627

GENERAL INFORMATION
Supporters Club Administrator: Ron Brown
Address: c/o Club
Telephone Number: (081) 974-8717
Car Parking: Yes
Coach Parking: Yes
Nearest Railway Station: Norbiton (1 mile)
Nearest Bus Station: Kingston
Club Shop: Yes
Opening Times: 1.00-5.00pm & 7.00-9.00pm
Telephone No.: (081) 547-3335
Postal Sales: Yes
Nearest Police Station: New Malden
Police Force: Metropolitan
Police Telephone No.: (081) 541-1212

GROUND INFORMATION
Away Supporters' Entrances: No Segregation
Away Supporters' Sections: No Segregation

DISABLED SUPPORTERS INFORMATION
Wheelchairs: Yes
Disabled Toilets: Yes
The Blind: No Special Facilities

ADMISSION INFO (1993/94 PRICES)
Adult Standing: £3.50
Adult Seating: £4.50
Child Standing: £1.50
Child Seating: £2.00
Programme Price: £1.00
FAX Number: (081) 947-5713

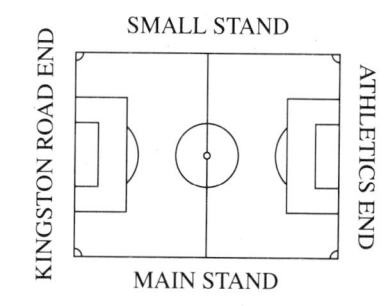

```
                    SMALL STAND
        ┌─────────────────────────────┐
  K     │                             │   A
  I     │                             │   T
  N     │                             │   H
  G     │                             │   L
  S     │                             │   E
  T     │                             │   T
  O     │                             │   I
  N     │                             │   C
        │                             │   S
  R     │                             │
  O     │                             │   E
  A     │                             │   N
  D     │                             │   D
        │                             │
  E     │                             │
  N     │                             │
  D     └─────────────────────────────┘
                    MAIN STAND
```

Travelling Supporters Information:
Routes: Take the A3 to New Malden, then north on the A2043 and left at roundabout and along to traffic lights. Turn left at the traffic lights entering Kingston on the London Road and follow the one-way system past the Norbiton Railway Station. Turn left into Richmond Road (A307) and ground is 0.5 mile along on the right.

MARLOW FC

Founded: 1870
Former Name(s): Great Marlow
Nickname: 'The Blues'
Ground: Alfred Davis Memorial Ground, Oaktree Road, Marlow, Bucks
Record Attendance: 10,000

Colours: Shirts - Royal Blue
Shorts - Royal Blue
Telephone No.: (0628) 483970
Daytime Phone No.: (0628) 483970
Pitch Size: 110 × 76yds
Ground Capacity: 3,000
Seating Capacity: 260

GENERAL INFORMATION
Supporters Club Administrator: Mrs J. Leslie
Address: c/o Club
Telephone Number: -
Car Parking: 100 Cars at Ground
Coach Parking: 2 Coaches at Ground
Nearest Railway Station: Marlow (1 mile)
Nearest Bus Station: High Wycombe
Club Shop: Yes
Opening Times: Matchdays Only 2.00-5.00pm (7.00-9.15pm evening matches)
Telephone No.: (0628) 483970
Postal Sales: Yes
Nearest Police Station: Marlow
Police Force: Thames Valley
Police Telephone No.: (0628) 898343

GROUND INFORMATION
Away Supporters' Entrances: Oak Tree Road
Away Supporters' Sections: -

DISABLED SUPPORTERS INFORMATION
Wheelchairs: Accommodated
Disabled Toilets: None
The Blind: No Special Facilities

ADMISSION INFO (1993/94 PRICES)
Adult Standing: £3.50
Adult Seating: £4.00
Child Standing: £2.00
Child Seating: £2.25
Programme Price: 80p
FAX Number: -

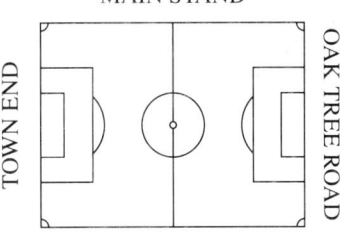

Travelling Supporters Information:
Routes: Take A404 to Marlow, turn off at A4155 intersection and follow into Town. Turn right into Maple Rise, Ground on Oaktree Road opposite.

MOLESEY FC

Founded: 1953
Former Name(s): None
Nickname: 'The Moles'
Ground: 412 Walton Road, West Molesey, Surrey
Record Attendance: 1,255 vs Sutton United (1966)

Colours: Shirts - White
Shorts - Black
Telephone No.: (081) 979-4823
Daytime Phone No.: (081) 979-4823
Pitch Size: 120 × 75yds
Ground Capacity: 4,000
Seating Capacity: 250

GENERAL INFORMATION
Supporters Club Administrator: None
Address: Social Club at Ground
Telephone Number: (081) 979-4823
Car Parking: At Ground
Coach Parking: At Ground
Nearest Railway Station: Hampton Court (1.25 miles)
Nearest Bus Station: Lord Hotham (100yds)
Club Shop: Yes
Opening Times: Matchdays Only
Telephone No.: (081) 979-4823
Postal Sales: Yes
Nearest Police Station: Molesey (1 mile)
Police Force: Metropolitan
Police Telephone No.: -

GROUND INFORMATION
Away Supporters' Entrances: No Segregation
Away Supporters' Sections: No Segregation

DISABLED SUPPORTERS INFORMATION
Wheelchairs: Accommodated
Disabled Toilets: Yes
The Blind: No Special Facilities

ADMISSION INFO (1993/94 PRICES)
Adult Standing: £3.50
Adult Seating: £4.00
Child Standing: £1.75
Child Seating: £2.00
Programme Price: 80p
FAX Number: (0727) 864296

```
                    MAIN STAND
        ┌──────────────────────────────┐
   OPEN │                              │ TERRACING
   TERRACING                           
        │                              │
        └──────────────────────────────┘
              THE BIKESHED
            COVERED TERRACING
```

Travelling Supporters Information:
Routes: Take A3 to the Hook underpass, then the A309 to the Scilly Isles roundabout and take 2nd exit into Hampton Court Way. Turn sharp left by Hampton Court Station into Bridge Road then right at next roundabout into Walton Road (B369). Ground is about 1 mile along on the left.

ST. ALBANS CITY FC

Founded: 1908
Former Name(s): None
Nickname: 'The Saints'
Ground: Clarence Park, Hatfield Road, St. Albans, Herts
Record Attendance: 9,757 (27/2/26)

Colours: Shirts - Blue & Yellow Stripes
Shorts - Blue
Telephone No.: (0727) 866819
Daytime Phone No.: (0582) 401487
Pitch Size: 110 × 80yds
Ground Capacity: 6,000
Seating Capacity: 900

GENERAL INFORMATION
Supporters Club Administrator: Andy Hammond
Address: 153 North Approach, Watford, Herts WD2 6EP
Telephone Number: (0923) 676851
Car Parking: Street Parking
Coach Parking: -
Nearest Railway Station: St. Albans City (200 yards)
Nearest Bus Station: City Centre (Short Walk)
Club Shop: Yes
Opening Times: Matchdays Only
Telephone No.: (0727) 866819
Postal Sales: Contact : Terry Edwards, 5 Wilshere Avenue, St. Albans, Herts
Nearest Police Station: Victoria Street, St. Albans
Police Force: Hertfordshire
Police Telephone No.: (0707) 276122

GROUND INFORMATION
Away Supporters' Entrances: No Segregation
Away Supporters' Sections: -

DISABLED SUPPORTERS INFORMATION
Wheelchairs: Accommodated - York Road entrance
Disabled Toilets: None
The Blind: No Special Facilities

ADMISSION INFO (1993/94 PRICES)
Adult Standing: £4.00
Adult Seating: £5.00
Child Standing: £2.50
Child Seating: £3.00
Programme Price: £1.00
FAX Number: (0727) 864296

```
              MAIN STAND
        ┌─────────────────────┐
HATFIELD│                     │YORK
ROAD    │                     │ROAD
END     │                     │END
        └─────────────────────┘
              TERRACING
```

Travelling Supporters Information:
Routes: Take the M1 or M10 to the A405 North Orbital Road and at the roundabout at the start of the M10 go north on the A5183 (Watling Street). Turn right along St. Stephen's Hill and carry along into St. Albans. Continue up Holywell Hill go through two sets of traffic lights and at the end of St. Peter's Street take right turn at roundabout into Hatfield Road. Follow over mini-roundabouts and at second set of traffic lights turn left into Clarence Road, ground on left. Park in Clarence Road and enter ground via park or in York Road and use entrance by footbridge.

43

STEVENAGE BOROUGH FC

Founded: 1976
Former Name(s): None
Nickname: 'Boro'
Ground: Stevenage Stadium, Broadhall Way, Stevenage, Herts   SG2 8RH
Record Attendance: 3,000 vs All Stars XI (May 1980)

Colours: Shirts - Red & White Stripes
             Shorts - Red
Telephone No.: (0438) 367059
Daytime Phone No.: (0438) 743482
Pitch Size: 110 × 70yds
Ground Capacity: 6,000
Seating Capacity: 500

GENERAL INFORMATION
Supporters Club Administrator: None
Address: -
Telephone Number: -
Car Parking: Spaces for 560 cars at ground
Coach Parking: At Ground
Nearest Railway Station: Stevenage (1 mile)
Nearest Bus Station: Stevenage
Club Shop: Yes
Opening Times: Matchdays Only
Telephone No.: (0438) 367059
Postal Sales: Yes
Nearest Police Station: Stevenage
Police Force: Hertfordshire
Police Telephone No.: -

GROUND INFORMATION
Away Supporters' Entrances: No Segregation
Away Supporters' Sections: No Segregation

DISABLED SUPPORTERS INFORMATION
Wheelchairs: Accommodated
Disabled Toilets: None
The Blind: No Special Facilities

ADMISSION INFO (1993/94 PRICES)
Adult Standing: £3.50
Adult Seating: £4.50
Child Standing: £1.80
Child Seating: £2.30
Programme Price: 70p
FAX Number: None

STAND

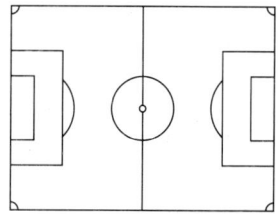

STAND & TERRACE

Travelling Supporters Information:
Routes: Exit A1(M) at junction 7 and take B197. Ground is on right at second roundabout.
Bus Routes: SB4 & SB5

SUTTON UNITED FC

Founded: 1898
Former Name(s): Sutton Guild Rovers
Nickname: 'U's'
Ground: Borough Sports Ground, Gander Green Lane, Sutton, Surrey SM1 2EY
Record Attendance: 14,000 (1970)

Colours: Shirts - Amber with Chocolate Trim
Shorts - Amber
Telephone No.: (081) 644-4440
Daytime Phone No.: (081) 644-5120
Pitch Size: 110 × 70yds
Ground Capacity: 6,100
Seating Capacity: 1,000

GENERAL INFORMATION
Supporters Club Administrator: Mark Frake
Address: 165 Ridge Road, Sutton, Surrey SM3 9LW
Telephone Number: (081) 641-2909
Car Parking: 150 Cars behind Main Stand
Coach Parking: 1 Coach in Car Park
Nearest Railway Station: West Sutton Adj.
Nearest Bus Station: -
Club Shop: Yes
Opening Times: Matchdays Only
Telephone No.: -
Postal Sales: Yes
Nearest Police Station: Sutton
Police Force: Metropolitan
Police Telephone No.: (081) 680-6212

GROUND INFORMATION
Away Supporters' Entrances: Collingwood Road
Away Supporters' Sections: Collingwood Road Terracing

DISABLED SUPPORTERS INFORMATION
Wheelchairs: Accommodated
Disabled Toilets: Yes
The Blind: No Special Facilities

ADMISSION INFO (1993/94 PRICES)
Adult Standing: £4.00
Adult Seating: £5.00
Child Standing: £2.00
Child Seating: £3.00
Programme Price: £1.00
FAX Number: (081) 644-5120

Travelling Supporters Information:
Routes: Exit M25 junction 8 (Reigate Hill) and travel North on A217 for approximately 8 miles. Cross A232 then turn right at next traffic lights (Gander PH) into Gander Green Lane. Ground 300 yards on left; From London: Gander Green Lane crosses Sutton Bypass 1 mile south of Rose Hill Roundabout. Avoid Sutton Town Centre especially on Saturdays.

WIVENHOE TOWN FC

Founded: 1925
Former Name(s): None
Nickname: 'Dragons'
Ground: Broad Lane, Elmstead Road, Wivenhoe, Essex CO7 7HA
Record Attendance: 1,922 (1990)

Colours: Shirts - Blue
Shorts - White
Telephone No.: (0206) 825380
Daytime Phone No.: (0279) 439181
Pitch Size: 120 × 75yds
Ground Capacity: 3,000
Seating Capacity: 500

GENERAL INFORMATION
Supporters Club Administrator: P. Reeve
Address: c/o Club
Telephone Number: (0206) 825380
Car Parking: 500 Cars at Ground
Coach Parking: At Ground
Nearest Railway Station: Wivenhoe (1 mile)
Nearest Bus Station: Wivenhoe
Club Shop: Yes
Opening Times: Matchdays Only
Telephone No.: (0206) 825380
Postal Sales: Yes
Nearest Police Station: Wivenhoe
Police Force: Essex
Police Telephone No.: -

GROUND INFORMATION
Away Supporters' Entrances: No Segregation
Away Supporters' Sections: No Segregation

DISABLED SUPPORTERS INFORMATION
Wheelchairs: Accommodated
Disabled Toilets: None
The Blind: No Special Facilities

ADMISSION INFO (1993/94 PRICES)
Adult Standing: £3.50
Adult Seating: £4.00
Child Standing: £1.75
Child Seating: £2.25
Programme Price: £1.00
FAX Number: None

Travelling Supporters Information:
Routes: Coming out of Colchester towards Clacton, take first turning towards Wivenhoe, ground is clearly visible on left turning towards Clacton (B1027)

WOKINGHAM TOWN FC

Founded: 1875
Former Name(s): None
Nickname: 'The Town', 'The T's'
Ground: Finchamstead Road, Wokingham, Berks
Record Attendance: 3,473 (1957/58)

Colours: Shirts - Amber
Shorts - Black
Telephone No.: (0734) 780253/772884
Daytime Phone No.: (0734) 780253
Pitch Size: 112 × 72yds
Ground Capacity: 5,000
Seating Capacity: 200

GENERAL INFORMATION
Supporters Club Administrator: None
Address: -
Telephone Number: -
Car Parking: Space for 250 Cars at Ground
Coach Parking: Yes at Ground
Nearest Railway Station: Wokingham (0.5 mile)
Nearest Bus Station: Bracknell
Club Shop: Yes
Opening Times: Matchdays Only
Telephone No.: n/a
Postal Sales: Yes
Nearest Police Station: Rectory Road, Wokingham
Police Force: Thames Valley
Police Telephone No.: (0734) 894440

GROUND INFORMATION
Away Supporters' Entrances: No Segregation
Away Supporters' Sections: No Segregation

DISABLED SUPPORTERS INFORMATION
Wheelchairs: Accommodated
Disabled Toilets: None
The Blind: Please Contact Club for Information

ADMISSION INFO (1993/94 PRICES)
Adult Standing: £4.00
Adult Seating: £4.50
Child Standing: £2.00
Child Seating: £2.00
Programme Price: £1.00
FAX Number: (0734) 890570

NEW FAR TERRACING
STATION END
TOWN END
MAIN STAND
Clubhouse

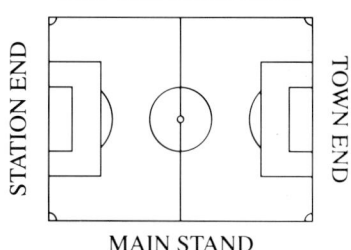

Travelling Supporters Information:
Routes: Exit M4 at junction 10 and follow signs to Wokingham. Alternatively exit M3 junction 3 and follow signs to Bracknell then Wokingham. Once in Wokingham keep left in Town Centre then follow A321 towards Sandhurst/Camberley. Straight over 2 small roundabouts, the ground is on the right, immediately after the Railway Bridge. Alternative route exit M3 junction 4 and follow signs to Wokingham. Go under the 1st Railway Bridge and the ground is immediately on the left before the second bridge.

YEADING FC

Founded: 1965
Former Name(s): None
Nickname: 'The Ding'
Ground: The Warren, Beaconsfield Road, Hayes, Middlesex
Record Attendance: 3,000 (1990)

Colours: Shirts - Red & Black Stripes
Shorts - Black
Telephone No.: (081) 848-7362
Daytime Phone No.: (081) 848-7362
Pitch Size: 115 × 72yds
Ground Capacity: 3,500
Seating Capacity: 250

GENERAL INFORMATION
Supporters Club Administrator: -
Address: -
Telephone Number: -
Car Parking: Spaces for 200 cars at ground
Coach Parking: At Ground
Nearest Railway Station: Hayes (2 miles)
Nearest Bus Station: Heathrow
Club Shop: None
Opening Times: -
Telephone No.: -
Postal Sales: -
Nearest Police Station: High Road, Southall
Police Force: Middlesex
Police Telephone No.: (081) 900-7212

GROUND INFORMATION
Away Supporters' Entrances: No Segregation
Away Supporters' Sections: No Segregation

DISABLED SUPPORTERS INFORMATION
Wheelchairs: Accommodated
Disabled Toilets: None
The Blind: No Special Facilities

ADMISSION INFO (1993/94 PRICES)
Adult Standing: £3.50
Adult Seating: £3.50
Child Standing: £1.75
Child Seating: £1.75
Programme Price: 80p
FAX Number: None

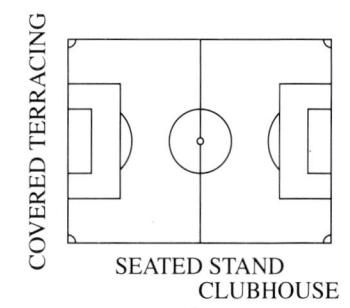

COVERED TERRACING

SEATED STAND
CLUBHOUSE

Travelling Supporters Information:
Routes: Exit M4 junction 4 and A312 past Hayes & Harlington Station. Cross the Grand Union Canal and continue to Uxbridge Road crossroad. Turn right along Uxbridge Road toward Southall about 0.75 mile and turn right at the traffic lights into Springfield Road then left into Beaconsfield Road - ground is on the right at the bottom.
Note: Do not approach from Southall end of Beaconsfield Road as there is no access because of the Grand Union Canal!

DIADORA LEAGUE DIVISION 1

ABINGDON TOWN FC
Founded: 1870 **Nickname**: 'The Town' **Former Name**: Abingdon FC. **Ground**: Culham Road, Abingdon OX14 3BT. **Ground Capacity**: 2,500 **Seating Capacity**: 325. **Tel. No**: (0235) 521684

BARKING FC
Founded: 1880 **Nickname**: 'The Blues' **Former Names**: Barking Rovers FC, Barking Victoria FC, Barking Town FC **Ground**: Mayesbrook Park, Lodge Avenue, Dagenham, Essex. **Ground Capacity**: 4,000 **Seating Capacity**: 200. **Tel. No**: (081) 599-2384

BERKHAMSTEAD TOWN FC
Founded: 1895 **Nickname**: 'The Lilywhites' **Former Name**: Berk'stead Comrades FC. **Ground**: Broadwater, Lower Kings Rd, Berkhamstead, Herts HP4 2AA. **Total Capacity**: 2,000 **Seating** : 200 **Tel.**: (0442) 863929

BILLERICAY TOWN FC
Founded: 1880 **Nickname**: 'Town' 'Blues' **Ground**: New Lodge, Blunts Wall Road, Billericay, Essex CM12 9SA. **Ground Capacity**: 3,600 **Seating Capacity**: 236. **Tel. No**: (0277) 652188

BISHOP'S STORTFORD FC
Founded: 1874 **Nickname**: 'Blues' ' Bishops' **Ground**: George Wilson Stadium, Rhodes Avenue, Bishop's Stortford, Herts. **Ground Capacity**: 4,500 **Seating Capacity**: 300. **Tel. No**: (0279) 654140; (0279) 652531 (Secretary)

BOGNOR REGIS TOWN FC
Founded: 1883 **Nickname**: 'The Rocks' **Ground**: Nyewood Lane, Bognor Regis, W.Sussex PO21 2TY **Ground Capacity**: 6,000 **Seating**: 230 **Tel. No**: (243) 822325

BOREHAM WOOD FC
Founded: 1946 **Nickname**: 'The Wood' **Former Name**: Boreham Wood Rovers FC, Royal Retournez FC. **Ground**: Meadow Park, Broughinge Road, Boreham Wood, Herts. **Ground Capacity**: 3,500 **Seating Capacity**: 250. **Tel. No**: (081) 953-5097; (081) 500-3902

CHALFONT ST. PETER FC
Founded: 1926 **Nickname**: 'The Saints' **Former Name**: Gold Hill FC. **Ground**: The Playing Fields, Amersham Road, Chalfont St. Peter, Bucks. **Ground Capacity**: 2,000 **Seating Capacity**: 100. **Tel. No**: (0753) 888583

CROYDON FC
Founded: 1953 **Nickname**: 'The Blues' **Former Name**: Croydon Amateurs FC. **Ground**: Croydon Sports Arena, Albert Road, South Norwood, London SE25 4QL. **Ground Capacity**: 8,000 **Seating Capacity**: 450. **Tel. No**: (081) 654-8555 (Club),   (081) 654-3462 (Ground)

HEYBRIDGE SWIFTS FC
Founded: 1882. **Nickname**: 'The Swifts' **Former Name**: Heybridge FC. **Ground**: Scraley Road, Heybridge, Maldon, Essex **Ground Capacity**: 2,000 **Seating Capacity**: 200. **Tel. No**: (0621) 852978; (0621) 854798

LEYTON FC
Founded: 1868 **Nickname**: 'Lilywhites' **Former Name**: Leyton-Wingate FC. **Ground**: Wingate-Leyton Stadium, Lea Bridge Road, Leyton, London. **Ground Capacity**: 1,500 **Seating Capacity**: 220. **Tel. No**: (081) 809-5057

MAIDENHEAD UNITED FC
Founded: 1869 **Nickname**: 'The Magpies' **Former Names**: Maidenhead FC amalgamated with Maidenhead Norfolkians FC in 1918 to form Maidenhead United FC. **Ground**: York Road, Maidenhead, Berks SL6 1SQ. **Ground Capac.**: 3,500 **Seating**: 200 **Tel.**: (0628) 36314

PURFLEET FC
Founded: 1985 **Nickname**: 'Fleet' **Ground**: Thurrock Hotel, Ship Lane, Grays, Essex RM15 4HB **Ground Capacity**: 3,500 **Seating** : 300 **Tel. No**: (0708) 868901

RUISLIP MANOR FC
Founded: 1938 **Nickname**: 'The Manor' **Ground**: Grosvenor Vale, Ruislip, Middlesex. **Ground Capacity**: 1,500 **Seating Capacity**: 175. **Tel. No**: (0895) 637487

STAINES TOWN FC
Founded: 1892 **Nickname**: 'The Swans' **Former Names**: Staines FC, Staines Vale FC, Staines Projectile FC, Staines Lagonda FC. **Ground**: Wheatsheaf Park, Wheatsheaf Lane, Staines, Middlesex TW18 2PD **Total Capacity**: 2,500 **Seating**: 250 **Tel.**: (0784) 455988

TOOTING & MITCHAM UNITED FC
Founded: 1932 **Nickname**: 'Terrors' **Former Names**: Tooting Town FC, Mitcham Wanderers FC. **Ground**: Sandy Lane, Mitcham, Surrey. **Ground Capacity**: 8,000 **Seating Capacity**: 1,900. **Tel. No**: (081) 651-2568 (Sec)

UXBRIDGE FC
Founded: 1871 **Nickname**: 'The Reds' **Ground**: Honeycroft, Horton Road, West Drayton, Middlesex UB7 8HX. **Ground Capacity**: 5,000 **Seating Capacity**: 201. **Tel. No**: (0895) 443757

WALTON & HERSHAM FC
Founded: 1896 **Nickname**: 'The Swans' **Ground**: Stompond Lane Sports Ground, Walton-on-Thames, Surrey KT12 1HF **Ground Capacity**: 6,500 **Seating Capacity**: 500. **Tel. No**: (0932) 245263; (0932) 782414

WEMBLEY FC
Founded: 1946 **Nickname**: 'The Lions' **Ground**: Vale Farm, Watford Road, Sudbury, Wembley, Middlesex HA0 4UR **Ground Capacity**: 4,000 **Seating Capacity**: 350. **Tel. No**: (081) 904-8169; (081) 908-3353 (Secretary)

WHYTELEAFE FC
Founded: 1946 **Nickname**: 'The Leafe' **Ground**: Church Road, Whyteleafe, Surrey. **Ground Capacity**: 5,000 **Seating Capacity**: 200. **Tel. No**: (081) 669-1672

WINDSOR & ETON FC
Founded: 1892 **Nickname**: 'The Royalists' **Ground**: Stag Meadow, St. Leonard's Road, Windsor, Berks SL4 3DR **Ground Capacity**: 4,500 **Seating Capacity**: 350 **Tel. No**: (0753) 860656

WORTHING FC
Founded: 1886 **Nickname**: 'The Rebels' **Ground**: Woodside Road, Worthing, West Sussex BN14 7QH **Ground Capacity**: 4,500 **Seating Capacity**: 450 **Tel. No**: (0273) 770921

DIADORA LEAGUE DIVISION 2

ALDERSHOT TOWN FC
Founded: 1992 Nickname: 'The Shots' Ground: Recreation Ground, High Street, Aldershot, GU11 1TW. Ground Capacity: 5,000 Seating Capacity: 1,885. Tel. No: (0252) 20211

AVELEY FC
Founded: 1927 Nickname: 'The Millers' Ground: Mill Field, Mill Road, Aveley, Essex RM15 4TR Ground Capacity: 8,000 Seating Capacity: 500. Tel. No: (0708) 865940; (0708) 555271 (Secretary)

BANSTEAD ATHLETIC FC
Founded: 1944 Nickname: 'The A's' Ground: Merland Rise, Tadworth, Surrey KT20 5JG. Ground Capacity: 3,000 Seating Capacity: 250. Tel. No: (0737) 350982; (081) 641-2957 (Secretary)

BARTON ROVERS FC
Founded: 1898 Nickname: 'Rovers' Ground: Sharpenhoe Road, Barton-le-Clay, Beds. MK45 4SD Ground Capacity: 4,000 Seating Capacity: 120. Tel. No: (0582) 882607; (0582) 882398 (Secretary)

CHERTSEY FC
Founded: 1890 Nickname: 'Curfews' Ground: Alwyns Lane, Chertsey, Surrey. Ground Capacity: 3,000. Seating Capacity: 200. Tel. No: (0932) 561774; (0276) 20745 (Secretary)

COLLIER ROW FC
Founded: 1929 Nickname: 'The Row' Former Names: Hampden United FC, Collier Juniors FC. Ground: Sungate, Collier Row, Romford, Essex Ground Capacity: 2,000 Seating Capacity: 120. Tel. No: (0708) 722766 (Ground), (0708) 768245 (Secretary)

EDGEWARE TOWN FC
Founded: 1939 Nickname: 'Wares' Ground: White Lion Ground, High Street, Edgware, Middlesex HA8 5AQ Ground Capacity: 4,500 Seating Capacity: 300. Tel. No: (081) 952-6799; (081) 863-4022 (Secretary)

EGHAM TOWN FC
Founded: 1896 (Reformed 1963) Nickname: 'Sarnies' Former Name: Egham FC. Ground: Tempest Road, Egham, Surrey. Ground Capacity: 3,000 Seating Capacity: 238. Tel. No: (0784) 435226; (0932) 783333

HAMPTON FC
Founded: 1920 Nickname: 'The Beavers' Ground: Beveree Stadium, Beaver Close, off Station Road, Hampton, Middlesex TW12 2BX. Ground Capacity: 2,000 Seating Capacity: 200. Tel. No: (081) 773-0858 (Sec)

HEMEL HEMPSTEAD FC
Founded: 1885 Nickname: 'Hemel' Former Name: Apsley FC. Ground: Vauxhall Road, Adeyfield, Hemel Hempstead, Herts. Ground Capacity: 2,500 Seating Capacity: 100. Tel. No: (0442) 259777

HUNGERFORD TOWN FC
Founded: 1886 Nickname: 'The Crusaders' Ground: Town Ground, Bulpit Lane, Hungerford, Berks RG17 0AY. Ground Capacity: 5,000 Seating Capacity: 130. Tel. No: (0488) 682939/684597

LEATHERHEAD FC
Founded: 1946 Nickname: 'Tanners' Ground: Fetcham Grove, Leatherhead, Surrey KT22 9AS Ground Capacity: 3,400 Seating Capacity: 200. Tel. No: (0372) 360151

LEWES FC
Founded: 1885 Nickname: 'Rooks' Ground: The Dripping Pan, Mountfield Rd, Lewes, E.Sussex Ground Capacity: 5,000 Seating Capacity: 300. Tel. No: (0273) 472100; (0273) 472822 (Secretary)

MALDEN VALE FC
Founded: 1967 Nickname: 'The Vale' Ground: Grand Drive, Raynes Park, SW20 9NB Ground Capacity: 3,000 Seating Capacity: 120. Tel. No: (081) 542-2193

METROPOLITAN POLICE FC
Founded: 1919 Nickname: 'The Blues' Ground: Metropolitan Police (Imber Court) Sports Club, Ember Lane, Thames Ditton, Surrey Ground Capacity: 3,000 Seating Capacity: 437. Tel. No: (081) 398-1267

NEWBURY TOWN FC
Founded: 1887 Nickname: 'The Town' Ground: Faraday Road, Newbury, Berks. Ground Capacity: 2,500 Seating Capacity: 100. Tel. No: (0635) 40048

RAINHAM TOWN FC
Founded: 1945 Nickname: 'Reds' Ground: Thurrock Hotel, Ship Lane, Aveley, Essex RM15 4HB Ground Capacity: 2,500 Seating Capacity: 305. Tel. No: (0708) 868901; (0708) 557596 (Secretary)

SAFFRON WALDEN TOWN FC
Founded: 1871 Nickname: 'Bloods' Ground: Caton's Lane, Saffron Walden, Essex CB11 3AD Ground Capacity: 5,000 Seating Capacity: 400. Tel. No: (0799) 522789; (0799) 550615 (Secretary)

THAME UNITED FC
Founded: 1883 Nickname: 'U's' Former Name: Thame FC, Thame Town FC. Ground: Windmill Road, Thame, Oxon. Ground Capacity: 2,000 Seating Capacity: 220. Tel. No: (0844) 213017; (0844) 237573

TILBURY FC
Founded: 1900 Nickname: 'The Town' Former Name: Abingdon FC. Ground: Chadfields, St. Chads Road, Tilbury, Essex Ground Capacity: 3,500. Seating Capacity: 200. Tel. No: (03752) 3093

WARE FC
Founded: 1892 Nickname: 'Blues' Ground: Buryfield, Park Road, Ware, Herts SG12 0AT Ground Capacity: 4,000. Seating Capacity: 200. Tel. No: (0920) 463247; (0992) 581862 (Secretary)

WITHAM TOWN FC
Founded: 1894 (re-formed 1948) Nickname: 'The Town' Ground: Spa Road, Witham, Essex CM8 1UN Ground Capacity: 2,000 Seating Capacity: 200. Tel. No: (0376) 500146; (0376) 512990 (Secretary)

DIADORA LEAGUE DIVISION 3

BRACKNELL TOWN FC
Founded: 1896 **Nickname**: 'The Robins' **Former Names**: Bracknell Wanderers FC **Ground**: Larges Lane, Bracknell, Berks. RG12 3AN **Ground Capacity**: 2,500 **Seating Capacity**: 150. **Tel. No**: (0344) 412305

CAMBERLEY TOWN FC
Founded: 1896 **Nickname**: 'Krooners' **Former Names**: Camberley FC, Yorktown FC & Camberley Wanderers FC. **Ground**: Krooner Park, Krooner Road, Camberley, Surrey, GU15 2QP. **Ground Capacity**: 2,500 **Seating Capacity**: 200. **Tel. No**: (0276) 65392 (Ground); (0483) 60829 (Secretary)

CHESHUNT FC
Founded: 1946 **Nickname**: None **Ground**: The Stadium Theobalds Lane, Cheshunt, Herts. **Ground Capacity**: 1,500 **Seating Capacity**: 150 **Tel.No**: (0992) 26752

CLAPTON FC
Founded: 1878 **Nickname**: 'Tons' **Former Names**: Downs Athletic FC **Ground**: The Old Spotted Dog Ground, Upton Lane, Forest Gate E7 9NP **Ground Capacity**: 2,000 **Seating Capacity**: 60. **Tel. No**: (081) 472-0822; (081) 591-5313 (Secretary)

COVE FC
Founded: 1897 **Nickname**: None **Ground**: Romayne Close, West Heath Road, Cove, Farnborough, Hants. **Ground Capacity**: 3,000 **Seating Capacity**: 100. **Tel. No**: (0252) 543615 (Ground), (0252) 518587 (Press Officer's Home)

EAST THURROCK UNITED FC
Founded: 1969 **Nickname**: 'Rocks' **Ground**: Rookery Hill, Corringham, Essex. **Ground Capacity**: 2,500. **Seating Capacity**: 160. **Tel. No**: (0375) 644166, (07082) 28818 (Secretary)

EPSOM & EWELL FC
Founded: 1917 **Nickname**: 'E's' **Former Names**: Epsom Town FC, Epsom FC. **Ground**: Merland Rise, Tadworth, Surrey KT20 5JG **Ground Capacity**: 3,000 **Seating Capacity**: 250. **Tel. No**: (0737) 350982; (0372) 729817 (Secretary)

FELTHAM & HOUNSLOW BOROUGH FC
Founded: 1946 **Nickname**: 'The Borough' **Former Name**: Feltham FC. **Ground**: The Arena, Shakespeare Avenue, Feltham. **Ground Capacity**: 10,000 **Seating Capacity**: 640. **Tel. No**: (0932) 739492 (Secretary's Home), (081) 890-6241 (Club), (081) 890-6905 (Ground)

FLACKWELL HEATH FC
Founded: 1907 **Nickname**: 'Heathens' **Ground**: Wilks Park, Heath End Road, Flackwell Heath, High Wycombe HP10 9EA **Ground Capacity**: 2,000 **Seating Capacity**: 150. **Tel. No**: (0628) 523892; (0628) 526204 (Secretary)

HAREFIELD UNITED FC
Founded: 1868. **Nickname**: 'The Hares'. **Ground**: Preston Park, Breakspeare Road North, Harefield, Middlesex UB9 6DG **Ground Capacity**: 2,000 **Seating Capacity**: 100 **Tel. No**: (0895) 823474

HARLOW TOWN FC
Founded: 1879 **Nickname**: 'The Owls' **Ground**: Harlow Sportcentre, Hammarskjold Road, Harlow, Essex. **Ground Capacity**: 10,000 **Seating Capacity**: 300. **Tel. No**: (0279) 444182

HERTFORD TOWN FC
Founded: 1908 **Nickname**: 'The Blues' **Ground**: Hertingfordbury Park, West St., Hertford, Herts SG13 8EZ. **Ground Capacity**: 6,500 **Seating Capacity**: 225. **Tel. No**: (0992) 583716 (Ground); (0992) 587011 (Secretary)

HORNCHURCH FC
Founded: 1923 **Nickname**: 'Urchins' **Former Names**: Upminster FC, Hornchurch & Upminster FC. **Ground**: The Stadium, Bridge Avenue, Upminster, Essex, RM14 2LX. **Ground Capacity**: 3,500 **Seating Capacity**: 300. **Tel. No**: (0708) 220080; (0708) 227891 (Secretary)

HORSHAM FC
Founded: 1885 **Nickname**: None **Ground**: Queen Street, Horsham RH13 5AD. **Ground Capacity**: 4,000 **Seating Capacity**: 300 **Tel. No**: (0403) 252310 (Ground); (0403) 264647 (Secretary)

KINGSBURY TOWN FC
Founded: 1944 **Nickname**: 'The Kings' **Ground**: Silver Jubilee Park, Townsend Lane, Kingsbury NW9 7NE **Ground Capacity**: 2,000 **Seating Capacity**: 165. **Tel. No**: (081) 205-1645

LEIGHTON TOWN FC
Founded: 1885 **Nickname**: 'The Reds' **Former Name**: Leighton United FC. **Ground**: Bell Close, Lake Street, Leighton Buzzard, Beds. **Ground Capacity**: 2,000 **Seating Capacity**: 162. **Tel. No**: (0525) 373311 (Ground)

NORTHWOOD FC
Founded: 1907 **Nickname**: 'The Woods' **Former Name**: Northwood Town FC **Ground**: Chestnut Avenue, Northwood, Middlesex. **Ground Capacity**: 1,750. **Seating Capacity**: 200. **Tel. No**: (0923) 827148

OXFORD CITY FC
Founded: 1882 **Nickname**: None **Former Names**: Pressed Steel FC **Ground**: Roman Way, Horspath Road, Cowley, Oxford **Ground Capacity**: 2,000 **Seating Capacity**: 150 **Tel. No**: (0865) 770163

ROYSTON TOWN FC
Founded: 1875 **Nickname**: 'The Crows' **Former Name**: Royston N.C. FC. **Ground**: Garden Walk, Royston, Herts. SG8 7HP **Ground Capacity**: 4,000 **Seating Capacity**: 300. **Tel. No**: (0763) 241204 (Ground)

SOUTHALL FC
Founded: 1871 **Nickname**: None **Ground**: Western Road, Southall, Middlesex UB2 5HX **Ground Capacity**: 10,000 **Seating Capacity**: 200. **Tel. No**: (081) 574-1084

TRING TOWN FC
Founded: 1904 **Nickname**: 'Tees' **Ground**: Pendley Sports Centre, Cow Lane, Tring, Herts **Ground Cap.**: 3,000 **Seating Capacity**: 200 **Tel. No**: (0442) 823075

ACCRINGTON STANLEY FC

Founded: 1876 (Reformed 1968)
Former Name(s): None
Nickname: 'Stanley' 'Reds'
Ground: Livingstone Road, Accrington, Lancashire
Record Attendance: 2,270 vs Gateshead (1992/93)
Colours: Shirts - Red
Shorts - White
Telephone No.: (0254) 383235
Daytime Phone No.: (0282) 864000 (P. Terry)
Pitch Size: 112 × 72yds
Ground Capacity: 2,420
Seating Capacity: 200

GENERAL INFORMATION
Supporters Club Administrator: Tony Clements
Address: 141 Manor Street, Accrington
Telephone Number: (0254) 393996
Car Parking: 150 Cars at Ground
Coach Parking: At Ground
Nearest Railway Station: Accrington (1.5 miles)
Nearest Bus Station: Accrington Town centre
Club Shop: Yes
Opening Times: Matchdays Only
Telephone No.: (0254) 383235
Postal Sales: Yes
Nearest Police Station: Manchester Road, Accrington
Police Force: Lancashire County
Police Telephone No.: (0254) 382141

GROUND INFORMATION
Away Supporters' Entrances: Bottom Car Park
Away Supporters' Sections: Car Park Side

DISABLED SUPPORTERS INFORMATION
Wheelchairs: Accommodated - Special Gate at Top Car Park
Disabled Toilets: None
The Blind: No Special Facilities

ADMISSION INFO (1992/93 PRICES)
Adult Standing: £3.00
Adult Seating: £3.00
Child Standing: £1.60
Child Seating: £1.60
Programme Price: £1.00
FAX Number: -

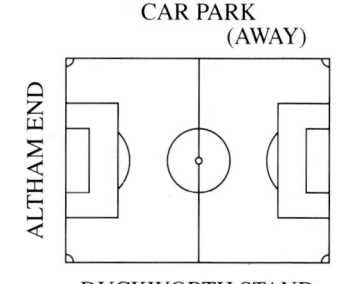

```
         CAR PARK
          (AWAY)
   ┌─────────────────┐
 A │                 │
 L │   ┌─────┐       │
 T │   │     │       │
 H │   │     │       │
 A │   │     │       │
 M │   └─────┘       │
   │                 │
 E │                 │
 N │                 │
 D │                 │
   └─────────────────┘
      DUCKWORTH STAND
```

Travelling Supporters Information:
Routes: Exit M66 onto A680 to Accrington. Travel through Town Centre, then turn right into Livingstone Road.

BARROW AFC

Founded: 1901
Turned Professional: 1908
Former Name(s): None
Nickname: 'Bluebirds'
Ground: Holker Street, Barrow-in-Furness, Cumbria
Record Attendance: 16,840 (1954)

Colours: Shirts - Royal Blue
Shorts - White
Telephone No.: (0229) 820346
Daytime Phone No.: (0229) 820346
Pitch Size: 110 × 75yds
Ground Capacity: 6,500
Seating Capacity: 1,250

GENERAL INFORMATION
Supporters Club Administrator: L. Barker
Address: 102 Scott Street, Barrow
Telephone Number: (0229) 823061
Car Parking: Street Parking, Popular Side Car Park and Soccer Bar Car Park
Coach Parking: Adjacent to Ground
Nearest Railway Station: Barrow Central (0.5 mile)
Nearest Bus Station: 0.5 mile
Club Shop:
Opening Times: Monday to Friday 9.30am - 4.00pm
Telephone No.: (0229) 823061
Postal Sales: Yes
Nearest Police Station: Barrow
Police Force: Cumbria
Police Telephone No.: (0229) 824532

GROUND INFORMATION
Away Supporters' Entrances: -
Away Supporters' Sections: None Specified

DISABLED SUPPORTERS INFORMATION
Wheelchairs: Accommodated
Disabled Toilets: None
The Blind: None

ADMISSION INFO (1993/94 PRICES)
Adult Standing: £3.50
Adult Seating: £5.00
Child Standing: £1.80
Child Seating: £2.50
Programme Price: £1.00
FAX Number: (0229) 871866
Social Club: (0229) 823839

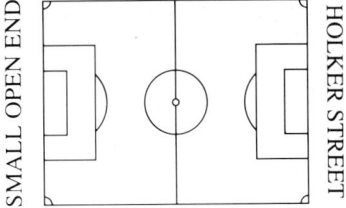

Travelling Supporters Information:
Routes: Exit M6 junction 36 and take A591 and A590 into Barrow-in-Furness. Turn right at Railway Station - Ground is about 0.5 mile further along.

BISHOP AUCKLAND FC

Founded: 1886
Former Name(s): None
Nickname: 'The Bishops' 'The Blues'
Ground: Kingsway, Bishops Auckland, Co. Durham
Record Attendance: 17,000 (1952/53)

Colours: Shirts - Light & Dark Blue
Shorts - Navy
Telephone No.: (0388) 604403
Daytime Phone No.: (0388) 608330
Pitch Size: 111 × 71yds
Ground Capacity: 5,000
Seating Capacity: 600

GENERAL INFORMATION
Supporters Club Administrator: A.J. Russell
Address: 21 Ramsey Crescent, Bishop Auckland, Co. Durham DL14 6TN
Telephone Number: (0388) 661568
Car Parking: Yes at Ground
Coach Parking: In Town
Nearest Railway Station: Bishop Auckland (0.5 mile)
Nearest Bus Station: Bishop Auckland
Club Shop: Yes
Opening Times: Matchdays Only
Telephone No.: (0388) 604403
Postal Sales: Yes
Nearest Police Station: Bishop Auckland
Police Force: County Durham
Police Telephone No.: (0388) 603566

GROUND INFORMATION
Away Supporters' Entrances: No Segregation Usual
Away Supporters' Sections: -

DISABLED SUPPORTERS INFORMATION
Wheelchairs: Accommodated by Arrangement
Disabled Toilets: None
The Blind: No Special Facilities

ADMISSION INFO (1993/94 PRICES)
Adult Standing: £2.50
Adult Seating: £3.00
Child Standing: £1.70
Child Seating: £2.20
Programme Price: 50p
FAX Number: -

```
         LIGHTFOOT              DELLWOOD
         TERRACE   MAIN STAND   TERRACE

    K
    I
    N
    G  T
    S  E
    W  R
    A  R
    Y  A
       C
       E

         CLUBHOUSE TERRACE
            (COVERED)
```

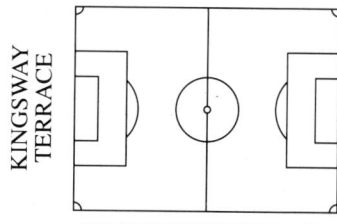

Travelling Supporters Information:
Routes: From South: A1 to Scotch Corner then follow signs to Bishop Auckland, Ground behind Town Centre; From North & West: M6 to A66 at Tebay then A66 to Barnard Castle. Follow signs to Bishop Auckland, Ground behind Town Centre.

BOSTON UNITED FC

Founded: 1934
Former Name(s): Boston Town/Boston Swifts
Nickname: 'The Pilgrims'
Ground: York Street, Boston, Lincolnshire
Record Attendance: 10,086 vs. Corby Town

Colours: Shirts - Amber with Black Trim
Shorts - Black
Telephone No.: (0205) 364406
Daytime Phone No.: (0205) 364406
Pitch Size: - 112 × 72 yds
Ground Capacity: 8,781
Seating Capacity: 1,769

GENERAL INFORMATION
Supporters Club Administrator: None
Address: -
Telephone Number: -
Car Parking: At Ground
Coach Parking: At Ground
Nearest Railway Station: Boston (0.5 miles)
Nearest Bus Station: Boston Coach Station (0.25 mile)
Club Shop: 14/16 Spain Place, Boston
Opening Times: Weekdays 9.00-4.30
Telephone No.: (0205) 364406
Postal Sales: Yes
Nearest Police Station: Boston
Police Force: Lincolnshire
Police Telephone No.: (0205) 366222

GROUND INFORMATION
Away Supporters' Entrances: Town End
Away Supporters' Sections: Town End Enclosure

DISABLED SUPPORTERS INFORMATION
Wheelchairs: Accommodated - York Street Stand
Disabled Toilets: None
The Blind: No Special Facilities

ADMISSION INFO (1993/94 PRICES)
Adult Standing: £3.50
Adult Seating: £4.00
Child Standing: £2.50
Child Seating: £3.00
Programme Price: £1.00
FAX Number: (0205) 354063

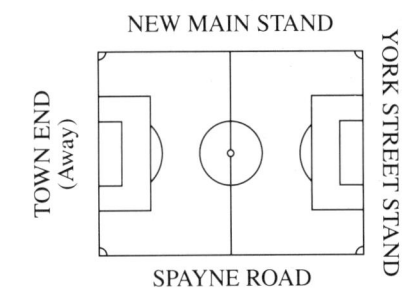

NEW MAIN STAND

TOWN END (Away)

YORK STREET STAND

SPAYNE ROAD

Travelling Supporters Information:
Routes: From North: Take A17 from Sleaford, bear right after railway crossing to traffic lights over bridge. Forward through traffic lights into York Street; From South & West: Take A16 from Spalding and turn right at traffic lights over bridge - forward through traffic lights into York Street.

BRIDLINGTON TOWN FC

Founded: 1925
Former Name(s): Bridlington Centrals United
Nickname: 'Town'
Ground: Queensgate Ground, Bridlington, YO16 5LN
Record Attendance: 2,102 vs Scarborough
Colours: Shirts - Red
Shorts - Red
Telephone No.: (0262) 670391
Daytime Phone No.: (0377) 241821
Pitch Size: - 110 × 76 yds
Ground Capacity: 7,794
Seating Capacity: 1,259

GENERAL INFORMATION
Supporters Club Administrator: Barry Garton
Address: c/o Club
Telephone Number: (0262) 850827
Car Parking: Large Car Park at Ground
Coach Parking: Car Park at Ground
Nearest Railway Station: Doncaster (1.5ml)
Nearest Bus Station: Doncaster
Club Shop: Yes - at ground
Opening Times: Matchdays Only
Telephone No.: c/o (0377) 241821
Postal Sales: Yes
Nearest Police Station: College Road, Doncaster
Police Force: South Yorkshire
Police Telephone No.: (0302) 366744

Note: Although the photograph is of the Queensgate Ground, the club are ground-sharing with Doncaster Rovers for the 1993/94 season.

GROUND INFORMATION
Away Supporters' Entrances: No Segregation
Away Supporters' Sections: No Segregation

DISABLED SUPPORTERS INFORMATION
Wheelchairs: Accommodated
Disabled Toilets: None
The Blind: No Special Facilities

ADMISSION INFO (1993/94 PRICES)
Adult Standing: £3.00
Adult Seating: £3.00
Child Standing: £1.50
Child Seating: £1.50
Programme Price: £1.00
FAX Number: None

POPULAR SIDE STAND

ROSSINGTON END (Away)

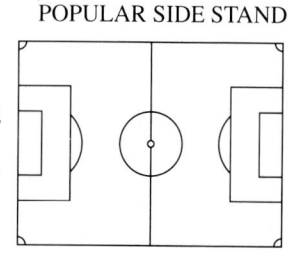

Enclosure
MAIN STAND
BAWTRY ROAD

BUS

Travelling Supporters Information:
Routes: From North: Take A1 to A638 into Town Centre, follow signs to Bawtry (A638), after 1.25 miles take 3rd exit from roundabout into Bawtry Road; From East: Take M18 to A630, after 2.75 miles take 1st exit at roundabout into A18, after 2.5 miles take 1st exit at roundabout into Bawtry Road; From South: Take M1 then M18, to A6182. After 2 miles 3rd exit at roundabout S/P 'Scunthorpe A18'. Then after 1.25 miles take 3rd exit at roundabout into Bawtry Road; From West: Take A635 into Town Centre and follow signs 'Bawtry' (then as South).

Buxton FC

Founded: 1877
Former Name(s): None
Nickname: 'The Bucks'
Ground: The Silverlands, Buxton, Derbyshire
Record Attendance: 6,000 (1962)
Colours: Shirts - White
Shorts - White
Telephone No.: (0298) 24733
Daytime Phone No.: (0298) 24733
Pitch Size: 112 × 70yds
Ground Capacity: 4,000
Seating Capacity: 585

GENERAL INFORMATION
Supporters Club Administrator: -
Address: -
Telephone Number: -
Car Parking: Street Parking
Coach Parking: Sylvan Park (200 yards)
Nearest Railway Station: Buxton (0.5 mile)
Nearest Bus Station: Buxton (0.25 mile)
Club Shop: Yes
Opening Times: Matchdays Only
Telephone No.: (0298) 24733
Postal Sales: Yes
Nearest Police Station: Buxton - Directly Opposite
Police Force: Derbyshire
Police Telephone No.: (0298) 72100

GROUND INFORMATION
Away Supporters' Entrances: No Segregation
Away Supporters' Sections: -

DISABLED SUPPORTERS INFORMATION
Wheelchairs: Accommodated
Disabled Toilets: Yes
The Blind: No Special Facilities

ADMISSION INFO (1993/94 PRICES)
Adult Standing: £3.50
Adult Seating: £3.50
Child Standing: £2.00
Child Seating: £2.00
Programme Price: 70p
FAX Number: (0298) 24733

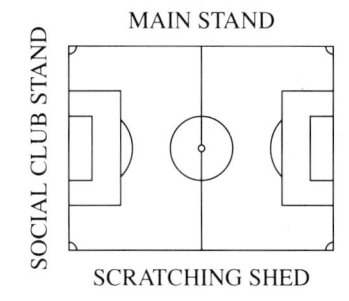

```
                MAIN STAND
        ┌──────────────────────┐
S       │                      │
O       │                      │
C       │                      │
I       │                      │
A       │                      │
L       │                      │
        │                      │
C       │                      │
L       │                      │
U       │                      │
B       │                      │
        │                      │
S       │                      │
T       │                      │
A       │                      │
N       │                      │
D       └──────────────────────┘
              SCRATCHING SHED
```

Travelling Supporters Information:
Routes: From South & East: Take A6 from Bakewell into Buxton and turn left at the traffic lights into Dale Road then right at the crossroads into the High Street. Turn third right into Hardwick Square and the ground is opposite the County Police Headquarters. From North & West: Take A6 from Stockport into Buxton, turn left at first traffic island towards Bakewell and turn right at second traffic island into Dale Road. Then as South & East.

CHORLEY FC

Founded: 1883
Former Name(s): None
Nickname: 'Magpies'
Ground: Victory Park, Duke Street, Chorley, PR7 3DU
Record Attendance: 9,679 (1931/32)
Colours: Shirts - Black & White Stripes Shorts - Black
Telephone No.: (02572) 63406
Daytime Phone No.: (02572) 63406
Pitch Size: 112 × 72yds
Ground Capacity: 4,400
Seating Capacity: 900

GENERAL INFORMATION
Supporters Club Administrator: -
Address: -
Telephone Number: -
Car Parking: 80 Cars at Ground
Coach Parking: At Ground
Nearest Railway Station: Chorley (0.25 ml)
Nearest Bus Station: 15 mins from Ground
Club Shop: Yes
Opening Times: Matchdays Only
Telephone No.: -
Postal Sales: Yes
Nearest Police Station: St. Thomas's Road, Chorley (10 minutes)
Police Force: Lancashire Constabulary
Police Telephone No.: (02572) 262831

GROUND INFORMATION
Away Supporters' Entrances: Ashby Street & Pilling Lane Stands
Away Supporters' Sections: Pilling Lane Stand

DISABLED SUPPORTERS INFORMATION
Wheelchairs: Accommodated by Arrangement
Disabled Toilets: Planned
The Blind: No Special Facilities

ADMISSION INFO (1993/94 PRICES)
Adult Standing: £3.00
Adult Seating: £4.00
Child Standing: £1.50
Child Seating: £2.00
Programme Price: 70p
FAX Number: (02572) 41195

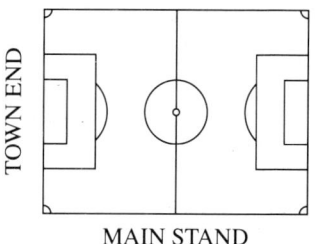

Travelling Supporters Information:
Routes: Exit M61 junction 6 and follow A6 to Chorley. Going past the Yarrow Bridge Hotel on Bolton Road, turn left at 1st set of lights into Pilling Lane. Take 1st right into Ashby Street, Ground 2nd entrance on left. Alternative Route: Exit M6 junction 27 and follow signs to Chorley. Turn left at lights and continue down the A49 for 2.5 miles before turning right onto B5251. On entering Chorley turn right into Duke Street 200 yards past The Plough.

COLWYN BAY FC

Founded: 1885
Former Name(s): None
Nickname: 'Bay' or 'Seagulls'
Ground: c/o Thornton Road Stadium, Ellesmere Port, South Wirral
Correspondence Address: 15 Smith Avenue, Old Colwyn, Clwyd   LL29 8BE

Colours: Shirts - Sky Blue
            Shorts - Maroon
Telephone No.: (0492) 516941
Daytime Phone No.: (0492) 515133
Pitch Size: 110 × 75yds
Ground Capacity: 5,000
Seating Capacity: 300

GENERAL INFORMATION
Supporters Club Administrator: None
Address: -
Telephone Number: -
Car Parking: At Ground
Coach Parking: At Ground
Nearest Railway Station: Chester (10 miles)
Nearest Bus Station: Ellesmere
Club Shop: Yes at Ground
Opening Times: Matchdays only
Telephone No.: (0492) 515133 (Not Matchdays)
Postal Sales: Yes
Nearest Police Station: Ellesmere Port
Police Force: Merseyside
Police Telephone No.: -

Note : The photograph shown is that of Colwyn Bay's own ground at Llanelian Road, Old Colwyn, but for the 1993/94 Season they are ground-sharing with Ellesmere Port Town FC at their Thornton Road Stadium.

GROUND INFORMATION
Away Supporters' Entrances: No Segregation
Away Supporters' Sections: No Segregation

DISABLED SUPPORTERS INFORMATION
Wheelchairs: Accommodated
Disabled Toilets: None
The Blind: No Special Facilities

ADMISSION INFO (1993/94 PRICES)
Adult Standing: £3.00
Adult Seating: £3.00
Child Standing: £1.50
Child Seating: £1.50
Programme Price: 60p
FAX Number: None

COVERED STAND

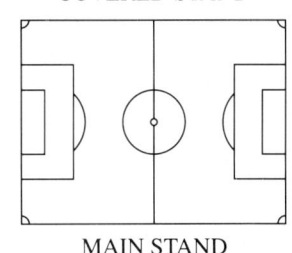

MAIN STAND

Travelling Supporters Information:
Routes: Take M56 to M53 to Ellesmere Port and exit at junction 10 onto the A5117 signposted Queensferry. Then take B5132 signposted to Ellesmere Port centre, after approximately 1 mile turn right following Thornton Road Industrial Estate and Stadium signs to Wolverham Road. Carry along across roundabout to bottom of road turn right into Thornton Road, Stadium 0.25 mile on the left.

DROYLSDEN FC

Founded: 1892
Former Name(s): None
Nickname: 'The Bloods'
Ground: Butchers Arms, Market Street, Droylsden, Manchester
Record Attendance: 5,000
Colours: Shirts - Red
Shorts - Red
Telephone No.: (061) 370-1426
Daytime Phone No.: (061) 370-1426
Pitch Size: 118 × 78yds
Ground Capacity: 3,500
Seating Capacity: 450

GENERAL INFORMATION
Supporters Club Administrator: R Harris
Address: c/o Club
Telephone Number: -
Car Parking: 200 Cars at Ground
Coach Parking: At Ground
Nearest Railway Station: Droylsden
Nearest Bus Station: Ashton
Club Shop: Yes
Opening Times: Matchdays Only
Telephone No.: (061) 370-1426
Postal Sales: Yes
Nearest Police Station: Manchester Road, Droylsden
Police Force: Greater Manchester
Police Telephone No.: (061) 330-8321

GROUND INFORMATION
Away Supporters' Entrances: Greenside Lane
Away Supporters' Sections: No Segregation

DISABLED SUPPORTERS INFORMATION
Wheelchairs: Accommodated
Disabled Toilets: Yes
The Blind: No Special Facilities

ADMISSION INFO (1992/93 PRICES)
Adult Standing: £3.00
Adult Seating: £3.00
Child Standing: £1.50
Child Seating: £1.50
Programme Price: 60p
FAX Number: -

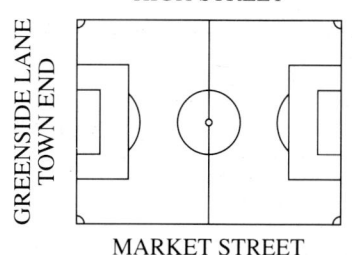

Travelling Supporters Information:
Routes: Take M62 to the end of M666 (Denton roundabout) for M56. Exit at the Denton/Ashton-under-Lyne turnoff following Droylsden signs (1-2 miles). Follow the road to the Manchester Road roundabout and along to the Traffic Lights at Market Street and turn right. Ground is 100 yards on the left.

EMLEY FC

Founded: 1903
Former Name(s): None
Nickname: None
Ground: Emley Welfare Sports Ground, Emley, Huddersfield, West Yorks.
Record Attendance: 5,139 (1/2/69)

Colours: Shirts - Sky Blue
Shorts - Maroon
Telephone No.: (0924) 848398 (Social Club)
(0924) 840087 (Matchdays Only)
Daytime Phone No.: (0484) 602720
Pitch Size: 110 × 70yds
Ground Capacity: 3,000
Seating Capacity: 250

GENERAL INFORMATION
Supporters Club Administrator: None
Address: -
Telephone Number: -
Car Parking: Spaces for 150 Cars at Ground
Coach Parking: At Ground
Nearest Railway Station: Huddersfield (7 miles)
Nearest Bus Station: Huddersfield
Club Shop: Yes
Opening Times: Matchdays Only
Telephone No.: (0924) 848398
Postal Sales: Yes
Nearest Police Station: Kirkburton
Police Force: West Yorkshire
Police Telephone No.: (0484) 436897

GROUND INFORMATION
Away Supporters' Entrances: None Specified
Away Supporters' Sections: -

DISABLED SUPPORTERS INFORMATION
Wheelchairs: Accommodated in Main Stand
Disabled Toilets: Yes
The Blind: No Special Facilities

ADMISSION INFO (1993/94 PRICES)
Adult Standing: £3.00
Adult Seating: £3.50
Child Standing: £2.00
Child Seating: £2.50
Programme Price: 60p
FAX Number: (0226) 762330

CRICKET GROUND SIDE
WARBURTON END
COVERED STANDING
THE ALEC HARDY STAND

Travelling Supporters Information:
Routes: Exit M1 junction 38 and follow signs to Huddersfield. Left at Roundabout onto Denby Dale Road A636 for approximately 0.75 mile then turn right, 1 mile to Emley. From West: Exit M62 junction 23 and follow road to Huddersfield. Take Ring Road out of Huddersfield following Wakefield signs for 5 miles, through Lepton, past White Horse Public House on left, turn right at the top of the hill, Emley is 2.75 miles.

FLEETWOOD TOWN FC

Founded: 1977
Former Name(s): Fleetwood FC (1907-77)
Nickname: 'The Fishermen'
Ground: Highbury Stadium, Park Avenue, Fleetwood, Lancashire
Record Attendance: 3,000 (1984-85)

Colours: Shirts - Red & White
Shorts - White
Telephone No.: (0253) 876443
Daytime Phone No.: (0253) 864763
Pitch Size: 108 × 75yds
Ground Capacity: 9,500
Seating Capacity: 300

GENERAL INFORMATION
Supporters Club Administrator: P. Jose
Address: 18 South Strand, Fleetwood
Telephone Number: (0253) 393448
Car Parking: 40 Cars at Ground
Coach Parking: At Ground
Nearest Railway Station: Poulton (7 miles)
Nearest Bus Station: Fleetwood
Club Shop: None
Opening Times: -
Telephone No.: -
Postal Sales: -
Nearest Police Station: Fleetwood
Police Force: Lancashire Constabulary
Police Telephone No.: (0253) 876611

GROUND INFORMATION
Away Supporters' Entrances: No Segregation
Away Supporters' Sections: -

DISABLED SUPPORTERS INFORMATION
Wheelchairs: Not Accommodated
Disabled Toilets: None
The Blind: No Special Facilities

ADMISSION INFO (1993/94 PRICES)
Adult Standing: £3.00
Adult Seating: £3.00
Child Standing: £2.00
Child Seating: £2.00
Programme Price: 60p
FAX Number: -

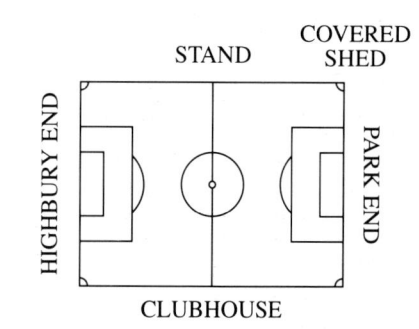

```
                    STAND      COVERED
                               SHED
  HIGHBURY END              PARK END
                 CLUBHOUSE
```

Travelling Supporters Information:
Routes: Exit M55 at junction 3 and follow A585 to Fleetwood. Immediately before the Town Centre, the fire station is situated on the left. Where the tramtracks cross the road, turn back on yourself for 100 yards, ground is behind the fire station.

FRICKLEY ATHLETIC FC

Founded: 1910
Former Name(s): Frickley Colliery FC
Nickname: 'The Blues'
Ground: Westfield Lane, South Emsell, Pontefract, West Yorks.
Record Attendance: 7,000 (1971)

Colours: Shirts - Blue
Shorts - Blue & White
Telephone No.: (0977) 642460
Daytime Phone No.: (0977) 643316
Pitch Size: 117 × 78yds
Ground Capacity: 6,000
Seating Capacity: 800

GENERAL INFORMATION
Supporters Club Administrator: H. Canner
Address: 18 Exchange Street, South Emsall, Pontefract, West Yorks.
Telephone Number: -
Car Parking: 200 Cars at Ground
Coach Parking: At Ground
Nearest Railway Station: South Emsall (2 miles)
Nearest Bus Station: South Emsall
Club Shop: Yes
Opening Times: Matchdays Only
Telephone No.: -
Postal Sales: Yes
Nearest Police Station: South Kirkby
Police Force: West Yorkshire
Police Telephone No.: (0977) 793611

GROUND INFORMATION
Away Supporters' Entrances: No Segregation
Away Supporters' Sections: -

DISABLED SUPPORTERS INFORMATION
Wheelchairs: Accommodated
Disabled Toilets: Yes
The Blind: Please contact Club for details

ADMISSION INFO (1993/94 PRICES)
Adult Standing: £2.50
Adult Seating: £3.00
Child Standing: £1.75
Child Seating: £1.75
Programme Price: 50p
FAX Number: -

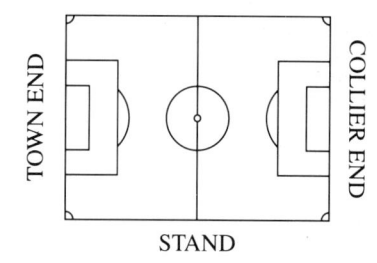

TOWN END / COLLIER END / STAND

Travelling Supporters Information:
Routes: From North: Follow A1 south leave A1 at first exit after Trusthouse Forte TraveLodge and follow road to South Kirkby then onto South Emsall. Upon entering the Town Centre take Westfield Lane then Oxford Street; From South: Take M1 to M18 to A1(M) and finally onto A638. Follow road towards Wakefield then follow road to South Emsall, then as above; From West & East: Take M62 to junction with A1 and head south to first exit, then as North.

GAINSBOROUGH TRINITY FC

Founded: 1873
Former Name(s): None
Nickname: 'The Blues'
Ground: The Northolme, North Street, Gainsborough, Lincolnshire
Record Attendance: 9,760 (1948)

Colours: Shirts - Blue
Shorts - White
Telephone No.: (0427) 613295
Daytime Phone No.: (0427) 612333
Pitch Size: 111 × 71yds
Ground Capacity: 9,500
Seating Capacity: 350

GENERAL INFORMATION
Supporters Club Administrator: T. Wallhead
Address: c/o Club
Telephone Number: (0427) 613688
Car Parking: Street Parking
Coach Parking: Opposite Ground
Nearest Railway Station: Lea Road (2 miles)
Nearest Bus Station: Heaton Street (1 mile)
Club Shop: Yes
Opening Times: Matchdays Only
Telephone No.: (0427) 613295
Postal Sales: Yes
Nearest Police Station: Morton Terrace (0.5 mile)
Police Force: Lincolnshire
Police Telephone No.: (0427) 810910

GROUND INFORMATION
Away Supporters' Entrances: No Segregation
Away Supporters' Sections: -

DISABLED SUPPORTERS INFORMATION
Wheelchairs: Not Accommodated
Disabled Toilets: None
The Blind: No Special Facilities

ADMISSION INFO (1993/94 PRICES)
Adult Standing: £3.00
Adult Seating: £3.00
Child Standing: £1.50
Child Seating: £1.50
Programme Price: 50p
FAX Number: -

CARLISLE STREET

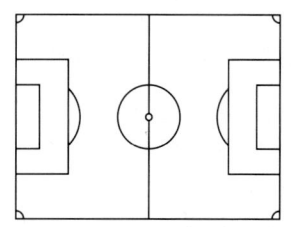

NORTH STREET

NORTHOLME

Travelling Supporters Information:
Routes: From North, South & West: Exit A1 near Worksop on to the A614 and take first left onto the B6420 to East Retford. Turn right on to A620 to Gainsborough and after 12 miles on outskirts of town take A631. Cross bridge, passing church and turn left along the A159. Pass Post Office and ground is 300 yards along North Street; From East: Take A631 into Gainsborough and turn left on to A159 then as North.

HORWICH R.M.I FC

Founded: 1896
Former Name(s): None
Nickname: 'Railwaymen'
Ground: Ramsbottom Road, Horwich, Lancs.
Record Attendance: 4,500

Colours: Shirts - Blue & White Stripes
Shorts - Blue
Telephone No.: (0204) 696908
Daytime Phone No.: (0204) 696908
Pitch Size: 112 × 75yds
Ground Capacity: 5,000
Seating Capacity: 400

GENERAL INFORMATION
Supporters Club Administrator: -
Address: -
Telephone Number: -
Car Parking: 60 Cars at Ground
Coach Parking: At Ground
Nearest Railway Station: Blackrod (1 mile)
Nearest Bus Station: Bolton
Club Shop: Yes
Opening Times: Matchdays Only
Telephone No.: (0204) 696908
Postal Sales: Yes
Nearest Police Station: -
Police Force: Lancashire
Police Telephone No.: -

GROUND INFORMATION
Away Supporters' Entrances: No Segregation
Away Supporters' Sections: No Segregation

DISABLED SUPPORTERS INFORMATION
Wheelchairs: Accommodated
Disabled Toilets: None
The Blind: No Special Facilities

ADMISSION INFO (1992/93 PRICES)
Adult Standing: £3.00
Adult Seating: £3.50
Child Standing: £1.50
Child Seating: £2.00
Programme Price: 50p
FAX Number: -

```
        COVERED TERRACE
    ┌─────────────────────┐
    │   ┌─┐         ┌─┐   │  C
    │   │ │         │ │   │  A
    │   │ │    ○    │ │   │  R
    │   │ │         │ │   │
    │   └─┘         └─┘   │  P
    │                     │  A
    └─────────────────────┘  R
                             K
         MAIN STAND
         CLUBHOUSE
         VICTORIA ROAD
```

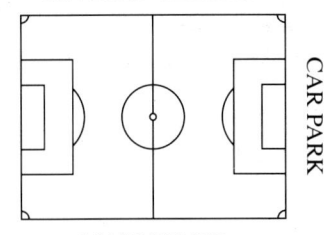

Travelling Supporters Information:
Routes: Exit M61 junction 6 and follow Horwich signs. Bear left at roundabout prior to second zebra crossing, then turn right onto Victoria Road. Ground situated to the left on a side road.

H YDE U NITED FC

Founded: 1919
Former Name(s): Hyde FC (1885-1917)
Nickname: 'Tigers'
Ground: Tameside Stadium, Ewen Fields, Walker Lane, Hyde, Cheshire SK14 2SB
Record Attendance: 9,500 (1952)

Colours: Shirts - Red
           Shorts - White
Telephone No.: (061) 368-1031 (Matchdays)
Daytime Phone No.: (061) 368-3687
Pitch Size: 120 × 70yds
Ground Capacity: 4,000
Seating Capacity: 400

GENERAL INFORMATION
Supporters Club Administrator: Ray Stanley
Address: 15 Balmain Avenue, Gorton, Manchester M18
Telephone Number: (061) 223-2445
Car Parking: 150 Cars at ground
Coach Parking: At Ground
Nearest Railway Station: Newton (0.25 ml)
Nearest Bus Station: Hyde
Club Shop: Yes
Opening Times: Matchdays Only
Telephone No.: (061) 368-1031
Postal Sales: Yes
Nearest Police Station: Hyde
Police Force: Tameside Area
Police Telephone No.: (061) 330-8321

GROUND INFORMATION
Away Supporters' Entrances: None Specified
Away Supporters' Sections: -

DISABLED SUPPORTERS INFORMATION
Wheelchairs: Accommodated
Disabled Toilets: Yes, behind Main Stand
The Blind: No Special Facilities

ADMISSION INFO (1992/93 PRICES)
Adult Standing: £3.00
Adult Seating: £3.50
Child Standing: £2.00
Child Seating: £2.50
Programme Price: 70p
FAX Number: -

NEW MAIN STAND

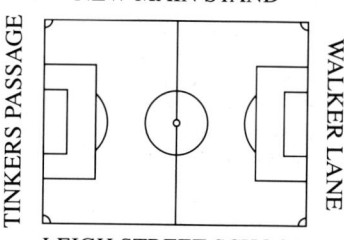

TINKERS PASSAGE

WALKER LANE

LEIGH STREET SCHOOL

Travelling Supporters Information:
Routes: On entering Hyde follow signs for Tameside Leisure Park. When on Walker Lane, take 2nd Car Park entrance near Leisure Pool and follow road round for Stadium.

KNOWSLEY UNITED FC

Founded: 1983
Former Name(s): Kirkby Town FC
Nickname: 'Altey Boys'
Ground: Alt Park, Endmoor Road, Huyton, Merseyside
Record Attendance: 900 vs Everton (1986)

Colours: Shirts - Red with Blue Trim
Shorts - Red
Telephone No.: (051) 480-2529
Daytime Phone No.: (051) 523-7317 (P. Orr)
Pitch Size: 112 × 75yds
Ground Capacity: 9,000
Seating Capacity: 300

GENERAL INFORMATION
Supporters Club Administrator: None
Address: -
Telephone Number: -
Car Parking: At Ground
Coach Parking: At Ground
Nearest Railway Station: Huyton (3 miles)
Club Shop: None at Present
Opening Times: -
Telephone No.: -
Postal Sales: -
Nearest Police Station: Huyton (3 miles)
Police Force: Merseyside
Police Telephone No.: -

GROUND INFORMATION
Away Supporters' Entrances: No Segregation
Away Supporters' Sections: No Segregation

DISABLED SUPPORTERS INFORMATION
Wheelchairs: Accommodated
Disabled Toilets: Only in Clubhouse
The Blind: No Special Facilities

ADMISSION INFO (1993/94 PRICES)
Adult Standing: £2.75
Adult Seating: £2.75
Child Standing: £1.50
Child Seating: £1.50
Programme Price: 50p
FAX Number: (051) 525-3165

MAIN STAND

CLUBHOUSE

OPEN TERRACING

(TRAINING PITCH) OPEN TERRACING

Travelling Supporters Information:
Routes: Exit M62 junction 6 and take M57 to junction 3. Follow signs for Huyton and at roundabout go straight across along Huyton Link Road. Ground is on left.

LEEK TOWN FC

Founded: 1952
Former Name(s): Abbey Green Rovers; Leek Lowe Hamil
Nickname: 'Blues'
Ground: Harrison Park, Macclesfield Road, Leek, Staffs ST13 8LD
Record Attendance: 3,048

Colours: Shirts - Blue
            Shorts - Blue
Telephone No.: (0538) 399278
Daytime Phone No.: (0782) 566241
Pitch Size: 115 × 80yds
Ground Capacity: 4,500
Seating Capacity: 400

GENERAL INFORMATION
Supporters Club Administrator: Neil Biddulph
Address: c/o Club
Telephone Number: (0538) 399278
Car Parking: 80 Cars at Ground
Coach Parking: At Ground
Nearest Railway Station: Stoke or Macclesfield (both 13 miles)
Nearest Bus Station: Leek
Club Shop: Yes
Opening Times: Matchdays Only
Telephone No.: (0538) 399278
Postal Sales: Yes
Nearest Police Station: Leek
Police Force: Staffordshire
Police Telephone No.: (0538) 399333

GROUND INFORMATION
Away Supporters' Entrances: Grace Street
Away Supporters' Sections: Grace Street Paddock

DISABLED SUPPORTERS INFORMATION
Wheelchairs: Accommodated
Disabled Toilets: Yes
The Blind: No Special Facilities

ADMISSION INFO (1993/94 PRICES)
Adult Standing: £3.50
Adult Seating: £4.00
Child Standing: £2.50
Child Seating: £3.00
Programme Price: 80p
FAX Number: (0538) 399826

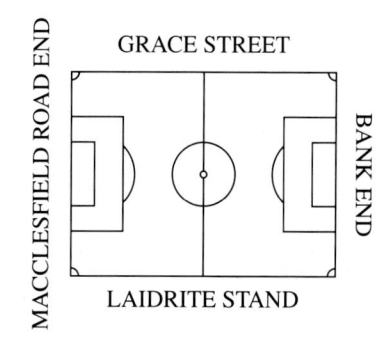

Travelling Supporters Information:
Routes: From North: Exit M6 at junction 17 to Macclesfield then follow A53 to Buxton Road; From South: Exit M6 at junction 15 to City Centre then follow A52 Leek Road. Ground is situated 0.5 mile outside Leek on Macclesfield side of the A53 Macclesfield to Buxton road.

Marine FC

Founded: 1894
Former Name(s): None
Nickname: 'Mariners' 'Lilywhites'
Ground: Rossett Park, College Road, Crosby, Liverpool L23 3AS
Record Attendance: 4,000 (1949)

Colours: Shirts - White
Shorts - Black
Telephone No.: (051) 924-1743/4046
Daytime Phone No.: (051) 924-1743
Pitch Size: 113 × 71yds
Ground Capacity: 3,000
Seating Capacity: 400

GENERAL INFORMATION
Supporters Club Administrator: Barry Lenton
Address: 16 Manor Avenue, Crosby, Liverpool L23 7YB
Telephone Number: (051) 924-1899
Car Parking: 60 Cars at Ground
Coach Parking: -
Nearest Railway Station: Blundell Sands & Crosby (800 yards)
Nearest Bus Station: Crosby
Club Shop: Yes
Opening Times: Matchdays Only
Telephone No.: (051) 924-4364
Postal Sales: Yes
Nearest Police Station: Crosby
Police Force: Merseyside
Police Telephone No.: (051) 709-6010

GROUND INFORMATION
Away Supporters' Entrances: Gate A
Away Supporters' Sections: -

DISABLED SUPPORTERS INFORMATION
Wheelchairs: Accommodated
Disabled Toilets: None
The Blind: No Special Facilities

ADMISSION INFO (1992/93 PRICES)
Adult Standing: £3.00
Adult Seating: £3.50
Child Standing: £2.00
Child Seating: £2.50
Programme Price: 60p
FAX Number: (051) 236-4453

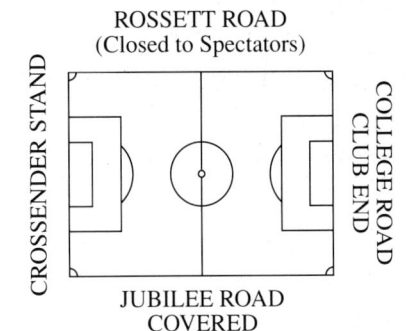

ROSSETT ROAD
(Closed to Spectators)

CROSSENDER STAND

COLLEGE ROAD
CLUB END

JUBILEE ROAD
COVERED

Travelling Supporters Information:
Routes: Follow M57/M58 Motorway to end. Follow signs into Crosby Town Centre, ground is situated on College Road which is off main Liverpool-Southport A565 road. Ground is sign-posted in town.

MATLOCK TOWN FC

Founded: 1885
Former Name(s): Hall Leys (pre-1900)
Nickname: 'The Gladiators'
Ground: Causeway Lane, Matlock, Derbyshire
Record Attendance: 5,123 (1975)
Colours: Shirts - Royal Blue
Shorts - White

Telephone No.: (0629) 55362 (Matchdays)
(0629) 583866 (24hr. Answerphone)
Daytime Phone No.: (0629) 583866
Pitch Size: 110 × 70yds
Ground Capacity: 3,200
Seating Capacity: 320

GENERAL INFORMATION
Supporters Club Administrator: Mrs. Susan Tomlinson
Address: M.T. Aux. Association, Causeway Lane, Matlock, Derbyshire
Telephone Number: (0629) 583866
Car Parking: 46 Cars at Ground
Coach Parking: Bus Station - Town Centre
Nearest Railway Station: Matlock (500 yds)
Nearest Bus Station: 350 yards
Club Shop: Yes
Opening Times: 9.00-4.00pm Weekdays, 9.00-12.00 Saturdays
Telephone No.: (0629) 583866
Postal Sales: Yes
Nearest Police Station: Matlock (500 yards)
Police Force: Derbyshire Constabulary
Police Telephone No.: (0629) 580100

GROUND INFORMATION
Away Supporters' Entrances: Matlock Green End
Away Supporters' Sections: Cyril Harrison Stand

DISABLED SUPPORTERS INFORMATION
Wheelchairs: Accommodated - Main Terracing
Disabled Toilets: Yes
The Blind: No Special Facilities

ADMISSION INFO (1993/94 PRICES)
Adult Standing: £3.00
Adult Seating: £3.50
Child Standing: £1.50
Child Seating: £2.00
Programme Price: 50p
FAX Number: None

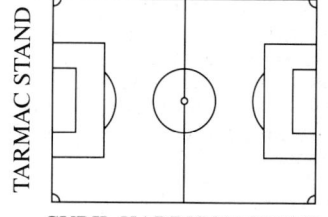

```
           MAIN STAND/TERRACING
        ┌─────────────────────────┐
T       │                         │  M
A       │                         │  A
R       │                         │  T
M       │                         │  L
A       │                         │  O
C       │                         │  C
        │                         │  K
S       │                         │
T       │                         │  G
A       │                         │  R
N       │                         │  E
D       │                         │  E
        │                         │  N
        │                         │
        │                         │  E
        │                         │  N
        └─────────────────────────┘  D
           CYRIL HARRISON STAND
```

Travelling Supporters Information:
Routes: Take the A6 to Matlock and at roundabout by the bus station take the A615 Alfreton Road. Causeway Lane is 500 yards along.

MORECAMBE FC

Founded: 1920
Former Name(s): Woodhill Lane (1920)
Nickname: 'Shrimps'
Ground: Christie Park, Lancaster Road, Morecambe   LA4 4TJ
Record Attendance: 10,000 (13/1/62)

Colours: Shirts - Red
Shorts - White
Telephone No.: (0524) 411797
Daytime Phone No.: (0524) 411797
Pitch Size: 118 × 76yds
Ground Capacity: 4,500
Seating Capacity: 700

GENERAL INFORMATION
Supporters Club Administrator: J. Corcoran
Address: c/o Club
Telephone Number: -
Car Parking: At Ground
Coach Parking: At Ground
Nearest Railway Station: Morecambe Central (0.5 mile)
Nearest Bus Station: Morecambe
Club Shop: Yes
Opening Times: Matchdays Only
Telephone No.: (0524) 411797
Postal Sales: Yes
Nearest Police Station: Morecambe
Police Force: Lancashire
Police Telephone No.: (0524) 411534

GROUND INFORMATION
Away Supporters' Entrances: Corner of South Terrace and Lancaster Road
Away Supporters' Sections: South Terrace

DISABLED SUPPORTERS INFORMATION
Wheelchairs: Accommodated in Disabled Stand
Disabled Toilets: Available for 1993/94 season
The Blind: No Special Facilities

ADMISSION INFO   (1992/93 PRICES)
Adult Standing: £3.00
Adult Seating: £3.50
Child Standing: £1.50
Child Seating: £1.75
Programme Price: 60p
FAX Number: (061) 320-4806

Travelling Supporters Information:
Routes: Exit M6 at junction 34. Then take A683 west in Lancaster and pick-up the A589 to Morecambe. At second roundabout on the outskirts of Morecambe, take 2nd exit into Lancaster Road and ground is on left, approximately 800 yards.

WHITLEY BAY FC

Founded: 1950
Former Name(s): Whitley Bay Athletic (1950-1958)
Nickname: 'The Bay'
Ground: Hillheads Park, Whitley Bay, Tyne & Wear
Record Attendance: 7,301

Colours: Shirts - Blue & White Stripes
Shorts - Blue
Telephone No.: (091) 2513680 (Ground)
(091) 2515179 (Secretary)
Daytime Phone No.: (091) 2515179
Pitch Size: 110 × 75yds
Ground Capacity: 4,500
Seating Capacity: 300

GENERAL INFORMATION
Supporters Club Administrator: Tom Moody
Address: 1 Haig Avenue, Whitley Bay
Telephone Number: (091) 2520087
Car Parking: Street Parking
Coach Parking: Outside Ground
Nearest Railway Station: Whitley Bay Metro (1 mile)
Nearest Bus Station: Whitley Bay (1 mile)
Club Shop: Yes
Opening Times: Matchdays Only
Telephone No.: -
Postal Sales: ?
Nearest Police Station: Whitley Bay
Police Force: Northumbria
Police Telephone No.: (091) 2323451

GROUND INFORMATION
Away Supporters' Entrances: Hillhead Road End
Away Supporters' Sections: Hillheads Road End

DISABLED SUPPORTERS INFORMATION
Wheelchairs: Accommodated in front of Office
Disabled Toilets: None
The Blind: No Special Facilities

ADMISSION INFO (1993/94 PRICES)
Adult Standing: £2.50
Adult Seating: £2.70
Child Standing: £1.20
Child Seating: £1.30
Programme Price: 50p
FAX Number: -

```
              MAIN STAND
         ┌─────────────────┐
HILLHEADS│                 │(HOUSING
ROAD END │                 │ ESTATE)
         └─────────────────┘
           FOXHUNTERS ROAD
```

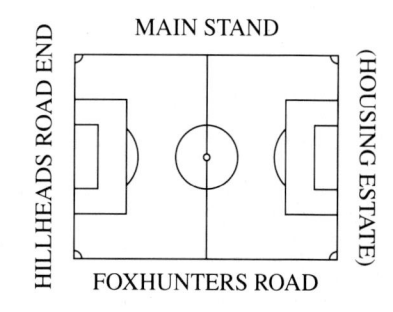

Travelling Supporters Information:
Routes: From South: A1-A19 through the Tyne Tunnel follow signs for Whitley Bay. Ground is behind Ice Rink; From West: A69 follow signs for the coast to Tynemouth then Whitley Bay. Ground is down Hillheads Road behind the Ice Rink.

WINSFORD UNITED FC

Founded: 1883
Former Name(s): Over Wanderers FC (prior to 1914)
Nickname: 'Blues'
Ground: Barton Stadium, Wharton, Winsford, Cheshire   CW7 3EU
Record Attendance: 7,000 (1947)

Colours: Shirts - Royal Blue
Shorts - White
Telephone No.: (0606) 593772
Daytime Phone No.: (0606) 593772
Pitch Size: 112 × 75yds
Ground Capacity: 7,000
Seating Capacity: 600

GENERAL INFORMATION
Supporters Club Administrator: G. Fuller
Address: c/o Club
Telephone Number: (0606) 593772
Car Parking: Space for 200 cars at ground
Coach Parking: At ground
Nearest Railway Station: Winsford (1 mile)
Nearest Bus Station: Northwich
Club Shop:
Opening Times: Matchdays Only
Telephone No.: (0606) 593772
Postal Sales: Yes
Nearest Police Station: Winsford
Police Force: Cheshire
Police Telephone No.: (0606) 592222

GROUND INFORMATION
Away Supporters' Entrances: No usual segregation
Away Supporters' Sections: Big games only

DISABLED SUPPORTERS INFORMATION
Wheelchairs: Not accommodated
Disabled Toilets: None
The Blind: No Special Facilities

ADMISSION INFO (1992/93 PRICES)
Adult Standing: £3.00
Adult Seating: £3.50
Child Standing: £1.50
Child Seating: £2.00
Programme Price: 50p
FAX Number: (0606) 552246

Travelling Supporters Information:
Routes: From North: Exit M6 at junction 19 and take A556 towards Northwich and Davenham, then follow A5018 to Winsford; From South: Exit M6 at junction 18 and follow A54 through Middlewich to Winsford. Turn off main road opposite lakeside park into Wharton Road and bear left. Ground is 0.25 mile along on the right.

NORTHERN PREMIER - DIVISION 1

ALFRETON TOWN FC
Founded: 1959 **Nickname**: None **Ground**: North Street, Alfreton, Derby **Ground Capacity**: 5,000 **Seating Capacity**: 172. **Tel. No**: (0773) 830277

ASHTON UNITED FC
Founded: 1878. **Nickname**: 'The Robins' **Former Name**: Hurst FC. **Ground**: Surrey Street, Hurst Cross, Ashton-under-Lyne, OL6 8DY **Ground Capacity**: 4,000 **Seating Capacity**: 250 **Tel. No**: (061) 339-9987 (Sec)

BAMBER BRIDGE FC
Founded: 1952 **Nickname**: 'The Brig' **Ground**: Irongate, Brownedge Road, Bamber Bridge, Preston, Lancs. **Ground Capacity**: 3,000 **Seating Capacity**: 220. **Tel. No**: (0772) 627387

CAERNARFON TOWN FC
Founded: 1876. **Nickname**: 'Canaries' **Former Names**: Caernarvon Athletic FC, Caernarvon Ironopolis FC, Caernarvon United FC **Ground**: Sharing at 'National Park', Katherine Street, Ashton-under-Lyne, Lancashire. **Ground Capacity**: 3,000. **Seating Capacity**: 350. **Tel. No**: (0286) 674045 (Secretary)

CITY OF LANCASTER FC
Founded: 1902. **Nickname**: 'Dolly Blues'. **Former Names**: Lancaster Town FC, Lancaster City FC **Ground**: Giant Axe, West Road, Lancaster. **Ground Capacity**: 5,000 **Seating Capacity**: 450 **Tel. No**: (0524) 35774

CONGLETON TOWN FC
Founded: 1901. **Nickname**: 'Bears' **Former Name**: Congleton Hornets FC **Ground**: Booth Street Ground, Crescent Road, Congleton, Cheshire. **Ground Capacity**: 3,000. **Seating Capacity**: 200. **Tel. No**: (0260) 274460

CURZON ASHTON FC
Founded: 1963. **Nickname**: 'Curzon'. **Ground**: 'National Park', Katherine Street, Ashton-under-Lyne, Lancs. **Ground Capacity**: 3,000. **Seating Capacity**: 350. **Tel. No**: (061) 330-6053

EASTWOOD TOWN FC
Founded: 1953. **Nickname**: 'The Badgers' **Ground**: Coronation Park, Eastwood, Notts. **Ground Capacity**: 6,700. **Seating Capacity**: 200. **Tel. No**: (0773) 715550

FARSLEY CELTIC AFC
Founded: 1908. **Nickname**: 'Celts' or 'Villagers' **Ground**: Throstle Nest, Newlands LS28 5BE **Ground Capacity**: 5,000. **Seating Capacity**: 200. **Tel. No**: (0532) 561517

GOOLE TOWN FC
Founded: 1900 **Nickname**: 'Vikings' **Ground**: Victoria Pleasure Grounds, Carter Street, Goole, N. Humberside **Ground Capacity**: 4,500 **Seating Capacity**: 200 **Tel. No**: (0405) 762794

GREAT HARWOOD TOWN FC
Founded: 1978. **Nickname**: 'Arrad'. **Ground**: The Showground, Wood Street, Great Harwood, Lancs. **Ground Capacity**: 2,800. **Seating Capacity**: 270. **Tel. No**: (0254) 883913

GRETNA FC
Founded: 1946. **Nickname**: 'Black & Whites' **Ground**: Raydale Park, Dominion Road, Gretna, Carlisle **Ground Capacity**: 2,200. **Seating Capacity**: 500. **Tel. No**: (0461) 37602

GUISELEY AFC
Founded: 1920 **Nickname**: None **Ground**: Nethermoor, Otley Road, Guiseley. **Ground Capacity**: 3,000. **Seating Capacity**: 370. **Tel. No**: (0943) 872872

HARROGATE TOWN FC
Founded: 1919. **Nickname**: 'The Sulphurites' **Former Names**: Harrogate FC & Harrogate Hotspurs FC. **Ground**: Wetherby Road, Harrogate. **Ground Capacity**: 3,850. **Seating Capacity**: 420. **Tel. No**: (0423) 883671

MOSSLEY FC
Founded: 1903 **Nickname**: 'The Lilywhites' **Former Names**: Park Villa FC, Mossley Juniors FC. **Ground**: Seel Park, Market Street, Mossley, Ashton-under-Lyne, Lancashire. **Ground Capacity**: 8,000 **Seating Capacity**: 200 **Tel. No**: (0457) 832369

NETHERFIELD AFC
Founded: 1920. **Nickname**: 'The Field'. **Ground**: Parkside, Parkside Road, Kendal. **Ground Capacity**: 4,750. **Seating Capacity**: 250. **Tel. No**: (0539) 726488

RADCLIFFE BOROUGH FC
Founded: 1949 **Nickname**: 'Boro' **Ground**: Stainton Park, Pilkington Road, Radcliffe, Manchester, M26 0PE. **Ground Capacity**: 3,000. **Seating Capacity**: 260. **Tel. No**: (061) 725-9197

SPENNYMOOR UNITED FC
Founded: 1901 **Nickname**: 'Moors' **Ground**: Brewery Field, Durham Road, Spennymoor, Co. Durham. **Ground Capacity**: 7,500. **Seating Capacity**: 300. **Tel. No**: (0388) 815168

WARRINGTON TOWN FC
Founded: 1949. **Nickname**: 'Town' **Former Name**: Stockton Heath FC **Ground**: Cantilever Park, Loushers Lane, Warrington WA4 2RS **Ground Capacity**: 2,000 **Seating Capacity**: 200. **Tel. No**: (0925) 31932

WHITBY TOWN FC
Founded: 1893 **Nickname**: 'The Seasiders' 'The Blues' **Ground**: Turnbull Ground, Upgang Lane, Whitby. **Ground Capacity**: 4,500 **Seating Capacity**: 250. **Tel. No**: (0947) 604847

WORKINGTON AFC
Founded: 1884 **Nickname**: 'The Reds' **Ground**: Borough Park, Workington, Cumbria CA14 2DT **Ground Capacity**: 3,000. **Seating Capacity**: 300. **Tel. No**: (0946) 61380 (Secretary)

WORKSOP TOWN FC
Founded: 1893. **Nickname**: 'Tigers' **Ground**: Babbage Way, off Sandy Lane, Worksop. **Ground Capacity**: 2,500. **Seating Capacity**: 400. **Tel. No**: (0909) 501911

NORTHERN COUNTIES EAST PREMIER

ARMTHORPE WELFARE FC
Founded: 1926 (Disbanded 1974, Reformed 1976) **Nickname**: 'Welly' **Ground**: Church Street, Armthorpe, Doncaster. **Ground Capacity**: 2,000 **Seating Capacity**: 100. **Tel. No**: (0302) 832514

ASHFIELD UNITED FC
Founded: 1885 **Nickname**: 'Snipes' **Former Name**: Sutton Town FC. **Ground**: Lowmoor Road, Kirkby-in-Ashfield, Notts. **Ground Capacity**: 8,000. **Seating Capacity**: 200. **Tel. No**: (0623) 794281

BELPER TOWN FC
Founded: 1883 **Nickname**: 'The Nailers' **Ground**: Christchurch Meadow, Bridge Street, Belper, Derbys. **Ground Capacity**: 4,000 **Seating Capacity**: 250. **Tel. No**: (0773) 825549

BRIGG TOWN FC
Founded: 1864 **Nickname**: 'The Zebras' **Ground**: The Hawthorns, Hawthorn Avenue, Brigg **Ground Capacity**: 4,000 **Seating Capacity**: 250. **Tel. No**: (0652) 652767

DENABY UNITED FC
Founded: 1895 **Nickname**: 'Reds' **Ground**: Tickhill Square, Denaby Main, Doncaster **Ground Capacity**: 6,000 **Seating Capacity**: 250. **Tel. No**: (0709) 864042

ECCLESHILL UNITED SPORTS CLUB FC
Founded: 1948 (Reformed after war) **Nickname**: 'The Eagles' **Former Name**: Eccleshill United FC **Ground**: Plumpton Park, Kingsway, Wrose, Bradford BD2 1PN **Ground Capacity**: 2,220 **Seating Capacity**: 220. **Tel. No**: (0274) 638053

GLASSHOUGHTON WELFARE FC
Founded: 1964 **Nickname**: None **Former Name**: Anson Sports FC. **Ground**: Leeds Road, Glasshoughton, Castleford, West Yorkshire. **Ground Capacity**: 2,000 **Seating Capacity**: 100 **Tel. No**: (0977) 556257 (Sec)

HARROGATE RAILWAY ATHLETIC FC*
Founded: 1935 **Nickname**: 'The Rail' **Ground**: Station View, Starbeck, Harrogate, North Yorkshire. **Ground Capacity**: 3,000 **Seating Capacity**: Nil **Tel. No**: (0423) 885539 (Ground), (0423) 883104 (Social Club)

HUCKNALL TOWN FC
Founded: 1946 **Nickname**: None **Ground**: Watnall Road, Hucknall, Notts, NG15. **Ground Capacity**: 2,100 **Seating Capacity**: 100. **Tel. No**: (0602) 636888

LINCOLN UNITED FC
Founded: 1939 **Nickname**: None **Ground**: Ashby Avenue, Hartsholme, Lincoln. **Ground Capacity**: 1,750. **Seating Capacity**: 150. **Tel. No**: (0522) 690674

LIVERSEDGE FC
Founded: 1910 **Nickname**: 'The Sedge' **Ground**: Clayborn Ground, Quaker Lane, Hightown Road, Cleckheaton, West Yorks **Ground Capacity**: 2,000 **Seating Capacity**: Nil **Tel. No**: (0274) 862123 (Secretary)

MALTBY MINERS WELFARE FC
Founded: 1972 **Nickname**: 'The Miners' **Former Name**: 'Maltby Main' **Ground**: Muglet Lane, Maltby, South Yorkshire. **Ground Capacity**: 1,000 **Seating Capacity**: Nil. **Tel. No**: (0709) 549958

NORTH FERRIBY UNITED FC
Founded: 1934 **Nickname**: 'United' **Ground**: Church Road, North Ferriby, East Yorks. **Ground Capacity**: 2,600 **Seating Capacity**: 240 **Tel. No**: (0482) 634601

OSSETT ALBION FC
Founded: 1944 **Ground**: Queens Terrace, Dimple Wells Road, Osset, West Yorks. **Ground Capacity**: 3,000 **Seating Capacity**: 240. **Tel. No**: (0924) 275630 (Sec)

OSSETT TOWN FC
Founded: 1936 **Nickname**: 'Town' **Ground**: 'Ingfield', Prospect Road, Ossett, Wakefield. **Ground Capacity**: 3,500 **Seating Capacity**: Nil. **Tel. No**: (0226) 382415

PICKERING TOWN AFC
Founded: 1888 **Nickname**: 'The Pikes' **Ground**: Recreation Ground, Mill Lane, Pickering. **Ground Capacity**: 2,000 **Seating Capacity**: 120. **Tel. No**: (0751) 73448

PONTEFRACT COLLIERIES FC
Founded: 1958 **Nickname**: 'The Colls' **Ground**: Skinner Lane, Pontefract, West Yorks. **Ground Capacity**: 2,000 **Seating Capacity**: Nil. **Tel. No**: (0977) 707756

SHEFFIELD FC *
Founded: 1857 (Oldest Club in World) **Nickname**: 'Club' **Ground**: Don Valley Stadium, Worksop Road, Sheffield **Ground Capacity**: 25,000 **Seating Capacity**: 25,000 **Tel. No**: (0742) 344553 (Secretary)

STOCKSBRIDGE PARK STEELS FC
Founded: 1959 **Nickname**: 'Works' **Former Name**: Stocksbridge Works FC. **Ground**: Bracken Moor Lane, Stocksbridge, Sheffield. **Ground Capacity**: 1,650 **Seating Capacity**: 500. **Tel. No**: (0742) 882045

THACKLEY FC
Founded: 1930 **Nickname**: None **Former Name**: Thackley Wesleyians FC **Ground**: Dennyfield, Ainsbury Avenue, Thackley, Bradford. **Ground Capacity**: 4,500 **Seating Capacity**: 200. **Tel. No**: (0274) 615871

WINTERTON RANGERS FC
Founded: 1934 **Nickname**: 'Rangers' **Ground**: West Street, Winterton, Scunthorpe. **Ground Capacity**: 3,000 **Seating Capacity**: 200. **Tel. No**: (0724) 732628

* Either Sheffield FC or Harrogate Railway Athletic FC will be relegated during the 1993/94 season. At present it is not known which shall be relegated.

NORTHERN LEAGUE DIVISION 1

APPLETON COLLIERY WELFARE FC
Founded: - Nickname: None Ground: Welfare Park, Appleton, Hetton-le-Hole, Tyne & Wear. Ground Capacity: 2,000 Seating Capacity: Nil Tel. No: (091) 526-0080

BILLINGHAM SYNTHONIA FC
Founded: 1923 Nickname: 'Synners' Ground: The Stadium, Central Avenue, Billingham, Cleveland. Ground Capacity: 1,970 Seating Capacity: 370. Tel. No: (0642) 532348 (Press Box), (0642) 553601 ext. 5365 (Groundsman's Office)

BLYTH SPARTANS FC
Founded: 1897 Nickname: 'Spartans' Ground: Croft Park, Blyth, Northumberland. Ground Capacity: 8,000 Seating Capacity: 600 approx. Tel. No: (0670) 361057

BRANDON UNITED FC
Founded: 1972. Nickname: None. Former Names: Rostrons FC. Ground: Welfare Ground, rear of Commercial Street, Brandon. Ground Capacity: 4,000 Seating Capacity: 50. Tel. No: (091) 373-1304 (Secretary)

CHESTER-LE-STREET TOWN FC
Founded: 1972 Nickname: 'The Cestrians' Former Name: Chester-le-Street, Garden Farm FC. Ground: Points North, Chester Moor, Chester-le-Street, County Durham. Ground Capacity: 2,500 Seating Capacity: 200. Tel. No: (091) 388-3554

CONSETT AFC
Founded: 1899 Nickname: 'The Steelmen' Former Name: Consett Celtic FC. Ground: Belle Vue Park, Ashdale Road, Consett, Co. Durham. Ground Capacity: 9,000 Seating Capacity: 474. Tel. No: (0207) 503788

DUNSTAN FEDERATION FC
Founded: 1975 Nickname: None Ground: Federation Park, Wellington Road, Dunstan, Gateshead, Tyne & Wear. Ground Capacity: 2,500 Seating Capacity: 80 Tel. No: (091) 267-2250

DURHAM CITY AFC
Founded: 1918 (Reformed 1950) Nickname: 'The Citizens' Ground: Ferens Park, The Sands, Durham DH1 1JY. Ground Capacity: 6,000. Seating Capacity: 150. Tel. No: (091) 384-1991

FERRYHILL ATHLETIC FC
Founded: 1921 Nickname: 'The Hill' 'The Latics' Ground: Darlington Road, Ferryhill, Co. Durham Ground Capacity: 6,000 Seating Capacity: 400. Tel. No: (0740) 651937

GUISBOROUGH TOWN FC
Founded: 1973 Nickname: 'Priorymen' Ground: King George V Playing Fields, Howlbeck Road, Guisborough, Cleveland. Ground Capacity: 3,500 Seating Capacity: 150 Tel. No: (0287) 638993 (Secretary)

HEBBURN FC
Founded: 1988 Nickname: None Former Name: Hebburn Reyrolle FC. Ground: Hebburn S & S Club Ground, Victoria Road, West Hebburn, Tyne and Wear. Ground Capacity: 2,000. Seating Capacity: 20 Tel. No:(091) 483-5101

MURTON AFC
Founded: 1891 Nickname: 'Gnashers' Former Names: Murton Red Star FC, Murton Colliery Wanderers FC. Ground: Recreation Park, Church Lane, Murton, Co. Durham. Ground Capacity: 3,500 Seating Capacity: 100. Tel. No: (091) 5170814

NEWCASTLE BLUE STAR FC
Founded: 1930 Nickname: 'Star' Former Name: Blue Star Welfare FC. Ground: Wheatsheaf Sports Ground, Woolsington, Newcastle-upon-Tyne. Ground Capacity: 2,000. Seating Capacity: 250. Tel. No: (091) 286-0425

NORTHALLERTON TOWN FC
Founded: 1890 Nickname: None Former Name: Northallerton Alliance FC. Ground: Anderby Road, Romanby, Northallerton, North Yorkshire. Ground Capacity: 2,500 Seating Capacity: 150. Tel. No: (0609) 779686

SEAHAM RED STAR FC
Founded: 1973 Nickname: None Ground: Seaham Town Park, Seaham, County Durham Ground Capacity: 2,000 Seating Capacity: 80. Tel. No: (091) 513-0880

SHILDON FC
Founded: 1890 Nickname: None Ground: Dean Street, Shildon, Co. Durham. Ground Capacity: 4,000 Seating Capacity: 350. Tel. No: (0325) 316322

STOCKTON FC
Founded: 1965 Nickname: None Former Name: Stockton Cricket Club FC. Ground: Teesdale Park, Acklam Road, Thornaby. Ground Capacity: 2,500 Seating Capacity: 110. Tel. No: (0642) 584593

TOW LAW TOWN FC
Founded: 1890 Nickname: 'Lawyers' Ground: Ironworks Road, Tow Law, Bishop Auckland, County Durham. Ground Capacity: 3,000 Seating Capacity: 500. Tel. No: (0388) 731443

WEST AUCKLAND TOWN FC
Founded: 1893 Nickname: 'West' Ground: Darlington Road Ground, West Auckland. Ground Capacity: 2,500 Seating Capacity: 200. Tel. No: (0388) 833783

WHITBY TOWN FC *
Founded: 1893 Nickname: 'The Seasiders' 'The Blues' Ground: Turnbull Ground, Upgang Lane, Whitby. Ground Capacity: 4,500 Seating Capacity: 250. Tel. No: (0947) 604847

* At the time of going to print, Whitby Town FC appeared in the fixtures of both the Northern League and Northern Premier League Division 1 subject to a dispute to be arbitrated by the F.A.

BASS NORTH WEST COUNTIES DIVISION 1

ATHERTON LABURNUM ROVERS FC
Founded: 1954 **Nickname**: 'Laburnum's' **Former Name**: Laburnum Rovers FC. **Ground**: Crilly Park, Spa Road, Atherton, Greater Manchester. **Ground Capacity**: 4,000 **Seating Capacity**: 500. **Tel. No**: (0942) 883950

BACUP BOROUGH FC
Founded: 1888 **Nickname**: 'The Boro' **Former Name**: Irwell Springs FC. **Ground**: West View, Cowtoot Lane, Blackthorn, Bacup, Lancashire. **Ground Capacity**: 2,000 **Seating Capacity**: 500. **Tel. No**: (0706) 873664

BLACKPOOL ROVERS FC
Founded: 1936 **Nickname**: 'Rovers' **Ground**: School Road, Marton, Blackpool, Lancs. **Ground Capacity**: 1,000 **Seating Capacity**: 250. **Tel. No**: (0253) 60570

BOOTLE FC
Founded: 1953. **Nickname**: None. **Ground**: Bucks Park, Perimeter Road, Netherton, Bootle, L30 7PT. **Ground Capacity**: 4,000 **Seating Capacity**: 350 **Tel. No**: (051) 527-1851

BRADFORD PARK AVENUE FC
Founded: 1907 (Reformed 1988) **Nickname**: 'Avenue' **Ground**: McLaren Field, Town Street, Bramley, Leeds. **Ground Capacity**: 4,000 **Seating Capacity**: 1,500. **Tel. No**: (0532) 564842

BURSCOUGH FC
Founded: 1946 **Nickname**: 'The Linnets' **Ground**: Victoria Park, Mart Lane, Burscough, Ormskirk, Lancs. L40 0SD. **Ground Capacity**: 3,500 **Seating Capacity**: 300. **Tel. No**: (0704) 893237

CHADDERTON FC
Founded: 1947 **Nickname**: 'Chaddy' **Former Names**: Millbrow FC, North Chadderton Amateurs FC. **Ground**: 'Broadway', Andrew Street, Chadderton, Oldham, Lancs. **Ground Capacity**: 2,500 **Seating Capacity**: 200. **Tel. No**: (061) 678-9624 (Secretary)

CLITHEROE FC
Founded: 1877 **Nickname**: 'The Blues' **Former Name**: Clitheroe Central FC. **Ground**: Shawbridge, Pendle Road, Clitheroe, Lancs. **Ground Capacity**: 4,000 **Seating Capacity**: 200. **Tel. No**: (0200) 24370 (Secretary)

DARWEN FC
Founded: 1877 **Nickname**: 'Anchormen' **Ground**: Anchor Ground, Anchor Road, Darwen, Lancs. **Ground Capacity**: 4,000 **Seating Capacity**: 230. **Tel. No**: (0254) 773642 (Secretary's Home)

EASTWOOD HANLEY FC
Founded: 1946 **Nickname**: 'Blues' **Ground**: Berryhill Fields, Trentmill Road, Hanley, Stoke-on-Trent, Staffs. **Ground Capacity**: 2,500 **Seating Capacity**: 200. **Tel. No**: (0782) 279162

FLIXTON FC
Founded: 1960 **Nickname**: 'The Valley Roaders' **Ground**: Valley Road, Flixton, Manchester, M31 2RQ. **Ground Capacity**: 2,000 **Seating Capacity**: 200. **Tel. No**: (061) 747-9937

GLOSSOP NORTH END AFC
Founded: 1886 **Nickname**: 'The Hillmen' **Former Names**: Glossop AFC, Glossop N.E. **Ground**: Surrey Street, Glossop, SK13 9AJ. **Ground Capacity**: 2,239 **Seating Capacity**: 250. **Tel. No**: (0457) 863852

KIDSGROVE ATHLETIC FC
Founded: 1952 **Nickname**: 'Athletic' **Ground**: Hollinwood Road, Kidsgrove, Stoke, Staffs. **Ground Capacity**: 3,000 **Seating Capacity**: 400. **Tel. No**: (0642) 532348

MAINE ROAD FC
Founded: 1955 **Nickname**: 'The Blues' **Former Name**: City Supporters (Rusholme) FC. **Ground**: Manchester County F.A. Ground, Brantingham Road, Chorlton, Manchester M21 1TG **Ground Capacity**: 2,000 **Seating Capacity**: 200. **Tel. No**: (061) 226-9917

NANTWICH TOWN FC
Founded: 1884 **Nickname**: 'The Dabbers' **Ground**: Jackson Avenue, off London Road, Nantwich, Cheshire. **Ground Capacity**: 1,500. **Seating Capacity**: 150. **Tel. No**: (0270) 624098

NEWCASTLE TOWN FC
Founded: 1964 **Nickname**: 'Castle' **Former Name**: Parkway Manley FC. **Ground**: Lyme Valley Parkway Stadium, Clayton, Newcastle-under-Lyme, Staffs. **Ground Capacity**: 4,000 **Seating Capacity**: 300. **Tel. No**: (0782) 333445

PENRITH FC
Founded: 1894. **Nickname**: 'The Blues' **Ground**: Southead Road, Penrith. **Ground Capacity**: 3,000 **Seating Capacity**: 250. **Tel. No**: (0768) 62551 (Secretary)

PRESCOT AFC
Founded: 1884. **Nickname**: 'The Tigers' **Former Names**: Prescot Cables FC, Prescot Town FC. **Ground**: Sandra Park, Hope Street, Prescot, Merseyside. **Ground Capacity**: 2,000 **Seating**: 500. **Tel. No**: (051) 430-0507

ROSSENDALE UNITED FC
Founded: 1898 **Nickname**: 'The Stags' **Ground**: Dark Lane, Staghills Road, Newchurch, Rossendale. **Ground Capacity**: 2,200. **Seating Capacity**: 400. **Tel. No**: (0706) 215119

ST. HELENS TOWN AFC
Founded: 1903 (Reformed 1946) **Nickname**: 'The Town' **Ground**: Hoghton Road, Sutton, St. Helens, Merseyside. **Ground Capacity**: 4,400 **Seating Capacity**: 200. **Tel. No**: (0744) 812721

SALFORD CITY FC
Founded: 1940 **Nickname**: 'City' **Ground**: Moor Lane, Kersal, Salford, Manchester. **Ground Capacity**: 8,000 **Seating Capacity**: 600. **Tel. No**: (061) 792-6287

SKELMERSDALE UNITED FC
Founded: 1882. **Nickname**: 'The Skemmers' **Ground**: White Moss Park, White Moss Road, Skelmersdale, Lancs. **Ground Capacity**: 10,000 **Seating Capacity**: 250. **Tel. No**: (0704) 894504

ATHERSTONE UNITED FC

Founded: 1979
Former Name(s): None
Nickname: 'The Adders'
Ground: Sheepy Road, Atherstone, Warwickshire
Office Address: 19 Hathaway Drive, Nuneaton Warwicks
Record Attendance: 2,588

Colours: Shirts - Red & White
Shorts - Red
Telephone No.: (0827) 717829
Daytime Phone No.: (0203) 351188
Pitch Size: 115 × 80yds
Ground Capacity: 3,500
Seating Capacity: 353

GENERAL INFORMATION
Supporters Club Administrator: P. Bickley
Address: 40 Spon Lane, Grendon, Atherstone
Telephone Number: -
Car Parking: Adjacent to Ground
Coach Parking: Adjacent to Ground
Nearest Railway Station: Atherstone (1 ml)
Nearest Bus Station: Atherstone/Nuneaton
Club Shop: Yes
Opening Times: Matchdays Only
Telephone No.: -
Postal Sales: -
Nearest Police Station: Atherstone 200 yards
Police Force: Warwicks
Police Telephone No.: -

GROUND INFORMATION
Away Supporters' Entrances: Gipsy Lane
Away Supporters' Sections: Gipsy Lane

DISABLED SUPPORTERS INFORMATION
Wheelchairs: 2 Accommodated
Disabled Toilets: Yes
The Blind: No Special Facilities

ADMISSION INFO (1992/93 PRICES)
Adult Standing: £3.00
Adult Seating: £3.50
Child Standing: £1.50
Child Seating: £1.75
Programme Price: 70p
FAX Number: -

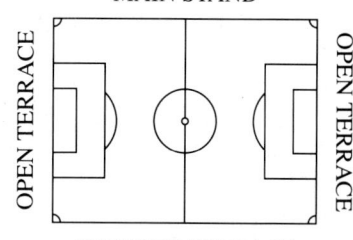

```
           MAIN STAND
      ┌─────────────────┐
   O  │                 │  O
   P  │                 │  P
   E  │                 │  E
   N  │                 │  N
      │                 │
   T  │                 │  T
   E  │                 │  E
   R  │                 │  R
   R  │                 │  R
   A  │                 │  A
   C  │                 │  C
   E  │                 │  E
      └─────────────────┘
        COVERED TERRACE
```

Travelling Supporters Information:
Routes: Take A5 into Town. Follow directions for Twycross Sheepy Magna - ground 0.5 mile on left.

BASHLEY FC

Founded: 1947
Former Name(s): None
Nickname: 'The Bash'
Ground: Recreation Ground, Bashley Common Road, New Milton, Hants
Record Attendance: 3,500

Colours: Shirts - Black & Gold
Shorts - Black
Telephone No.: (0425) 620280
Daytime Phone No.: (0920) 438849
Pitch Size: 110 × 70yds
Ground Capacity: 4,250
Seating Capacity: 400

GENERAL INFORMATION
Supporters Club Administrator: D. Groom
Address: c/o Club
Telephone Number: (0202) 558391
Car Parking: Yes
Coach Parking: Yes
Nearest Railway Station: New Milton
Nearest Bus Station: New Milton
Club Shop: Yes
Opening Times: Matchdays Only
Telephone No.: (0425) 620280
Postal Sales: Yes
Nearest Police Station: New Milton
Police Force: Hants
Police Telephone No.: (0425) 615101

GROUND INFORMATION
Away Supporters' Entrances: None Specifically
Away Supporters' Sections: None Specifically

DISABLED SUPPORTERS INFORMATION
Wheelchairs: Accommodated
Disabled Toilets: To be built
The Blind: No Special Facilities

ADMISSION INFO (1993/94 PRICES)
Adult Standing: £3.00
Adult Seating: £3.50
Child Standing: £1.50
Child Seating: £2.00
Programme Price: 70p
FAX Number: (0425) 638376

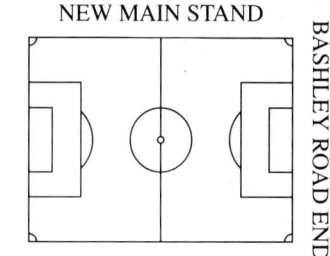

NEW MAIN STAND

BASHLEY ROAD END

Travelling Supporters Information:
Routes: From Southampton or M27: Take A35 Lyndhurst to Bournemouth Road. Turn left on to the B3058 Bashley - New Milton Road; From Bournemouth & West: Take A35 to Southampton then turn right on B3055 at Hinton Church. After 2 miles turn left at Bashley Crossroads towards the Ground.

BURTON ALBION FC

Founded: 1950
Former Name(s): None
Nickname: 'The Brewers'
Ground: Eton Park, Princess Way, Burton-on-Trent DE14 2RU
Record Attendance: 5,860 (1964)
Colours: Shirts - Yellow
Shorts - Yellow
Telephone No.: (0283) 65938
Daytime Phone No.: (0283) 65938
Pitch Size: 110 × 72yds
Ground Capacity: 8,000
Seating Capacity: 296

GENERAL INFORMATION
Supporters Club Administrator: Pete Thomas
Address: c/o Club
Telephone Number: (0283) 65938
Car Parking: At Ground (300 cars)
Coach Parking: At Ground
Nearest Railway Station: Burton-on-Trent (1 mile)
Nearest Bus Station: Burton-on-Trent (1 ml)
Club Shop: Yes
Opening Times: Matchdays Only
Telephone No.: (0283) 65938
Postal Sales: -
Nearest Police Station: Burton (1 mile)
Police Force: Staffordshire
Police Telephone No.: (0283) 65011

GROUND INFORMATION
Away Supporters' Entrances: Derby Road
Away Supporters' Sections: Derby Road

DISABLED SUPPORTERS INFORMATION
Wheelchairs: Access to terraces only - through Main Gate
Disabled Toilets: None
The Blind: No Special Facilities

ADMISSION INFO (1993/94 PRICES)
Adult Standing: £3.00
Adult Seating: £4.00
Child Standing: £1.00
Child Seating: £2.00
Programme Price: 60p
FAX Number: None

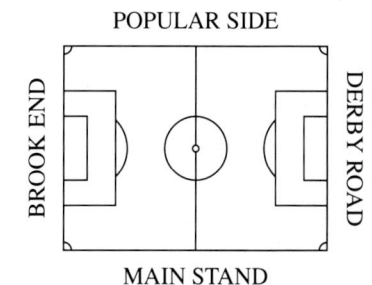

POPULAR SIDE
BROOK END
DERBY ROAD
MAIN STAND

Travelling Supporters Information:
Routes: From the North: Exit the M1 at junction 28 and follow the A38 towards Burton. Take the turning onto A5121 and follow into Burton. Turn right at the island and the ground is on the left; From South: Exit the M1 at junction 22 and follow the A50 towards Burton. Once in Burton go over Trent Bridge and through 3 sets of traffic lights. Turn right at the mini island and continue to the next island where turn left, entrance to the ground is on the left.

CAMBRIDGE CITY FC

Founded: 1908
Former Name(s): Cambridge Town FC
Nickname: 'City Devils'
Ground: City Ground, Milton Road, Cambridge   CB4 1UY
Record Attendance: 12,000 (1950)

Colours: Shirts - White
Shorts - Black
Telephone No.: (0223) 357973
Daytime Phone No.: (0223) 314632
Pitch Size: 110 × 71yds
Ground Capacity: 5,000
Seating Capacity: 495

GENERAL INFORMATION
Supporters Club Administrator: Clive Hilliar
Address: City Ground, Cambridge
Telephone Number: (0223) 357973
Car Parking: At Ground (200 cars)
Coach Parking: At Ground
Nearest Railway Station: Cambridge (2 mls)
Nearest Bus Station: Cambridge
Club Shop: Yes
Opening Times: Matchdays Only
Telephone No.: (0223) 357973
Postal Sales: Yes
Nearest Police Station: Park Side, Cambridge
Police Force: Mid Anglia
Police Telephone No.: (0223) 358966

GROUND INFORMATION
Away Supporters' Entrances: No Segregation
Away Supporters' Sections: No Segregation

DISABLED SUPPORTERS INFORMATION
Wheelchairs: Accommodated
Disabled Toilets: Yes
The Blind: No Special Facilities

ADMISSION INFO (1993/94 PRICES)
Adult Standing: £4.00
Adult Seating: £4.00
Child Standing: £2.00
Child Seating: £2.00
Programme Price: 50p
FAX Number: None

```
              ALLOTMENT SIDE
         ┌─────────────────────┐
W        │                     │        S
E        │                     │        C
S        │                     │        H
T        │                     │        O
B        │                     │        O
R        │                     │        L
O        │                     │
O        │                     │        R
K        │                     │        O
         │                     │        A
E        │                     │        D
N        │                     │
D        │                     │
         └─────────────────────┘
              MAIN STAND
              CLUBHOUSE
```

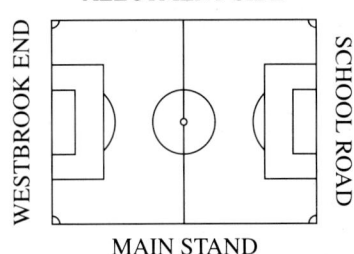

Travelling Supporters Information:
Routes: Exit M11 junction 13 and take A1303 into the city. At the end of Madingley Road, turn left into Chesterton Lane and then Chesterton Road. Go into the one-way system and turn left onto Milton Road (A10) - ground is on the left.

CHELMSFORD CITY FC

Founded: 1938
Former Name(s): Chelmsford FC (1878-1938)
Nickname: 'City'
Ground: The Stadium, New Writtle Street, Chelmsford, Essex   CM2 0RP
Record Attendance: 16,807   (10/9/49)

Colours: Shirts - White
   Shorts - Claret
Telephone No.: (0245) 353052
Daytime Phone No.: (0245) 353052
Pitch Size: 112 × 74yds
Ground Capacity: 2,850
Seating Capacity: 1,296

GENERAL INFORMATION
Supporters Club Administrator: D. Southwood
Address: 57 Heath Drive, Chelmsford, Essex   CM2 9HE
Telephone Number: (0245) 260186
Car Parking: Council Car Park adjacent to Cricket Ground End
Coach Parking: Street Parking
Nearest Railway Station: Chelmsford (0.5 mile)
Nearest Bus Station: Chelmsford (0.5 mile)
Club Shop: At Ground
Opening Times: One hour before games, half-time and 15 minutes after a game
Telephone No.: -
Postal Sales: Yes
Nearest Police Station: Chelmsford
Police Force: Essex
Police Telephone No.: (0245) 491212

GROUND INFORMATION
Away Supporters' Entrances: Usually no segregation
Away Supporters' Sections: Otherwise Wolseley End

DISABLED SUPPORTERS INFORMATION
Wheelchairs: Access via vehicle gates - Wolseley End
Disabled Toilets: None
The Blind: No Special Facilities

ADMISSION INFO (1993/94 PRICES)
Adult Standing: £4.00
Adult Seating: £5.00
Child Standing: £2.00
Child Seating: £2.50
Programme Price: £1.00
FAX Number: (0245) 495420

```
             OLD BARN ENCLOSURE
       ┌─────────────────────────────┐
  W    │                             │  C
  O    │                             │  R
  L    │                             │  I
  S    │                             │  C
  E    │                             │  K
  L    │                             │  E
  E    │                             │  T
  Y    │                             │
       │                             │  G
  E    │                             │  R
  N    │                             │  O
  D    │                             │  U
       │                             │  N
       │                             │  D
       └─────────────────────────────┘
             NEW WRITTLE STREET
```

Travelling Supporters Information:
Routes: From A12: Take A1016 (Chelmsford) exit and follow Colchester signs. At the 3rd roundabout, turn left onto B1007, New London Road. At the 2nd set of traffic lights turn left (signed County Cricket Ground). Ground is 100 yards on the right.

CHELTENHAM TOWN FC

Founded: 1892
Former Name(s): None
Nickname: 'Robins'
Ground: Whaddon Road, Cheltenham, Gloucestershire
Record Attendance: 8,326 (1956)

Colours: Shirts - Red & White Stripes
Shorts - Black with Red Trim
Telephone No.: (0242) 573558
Daytime Phone No.: (0242) 573558
Pitch Size: 110 × 73yds
Ground Capacity: 6,000
Seating Capacity: 1,200

GENERAL INFORMATION
Supporters Club Administrator: Mrs. Joan Bannister
Address: c/o Club
Telephone Number: (0242) 573558
Car Parking: At Ground (120 spaces)
Coach Parking: Wymans Road
Nearest Railway Station: Cheltenham Spa (2 miles)
Nearest Bus Station: Cheltenham Royal Well
Club Shop:
Opening Times: Matchdays Only & Office during week
Telephone No.: (0242) 521974
Postal Sales: Yes
Nearest Police Station: Whaddon, Cheltenham
Police Force: Gloucestershire
Police Telephone No.: (0242) 528282

GROUND INFORMATION
Away Supporters' Entrances: -
Away Supporters' Sections: None Specified

DISABLED SUPPORTERS INFORMATION
Wheelchairs: Accommodated
Disabled Toilets: None
The Blind: No Special Facilities

ADMISSION INFO (1993/94 PRICES)
Adult Standing: £3.50
Adult Seating: £5.00 and £6.00
Child Standing: £2.50
Child Seating: £3.00 and £4.00
Programme Price: 80p
FAX Number: (0242) 224675

WYMANS ROAD SIDE

PRESTBURY ROAD

WHADDON ROAD END

MAIN STAND & CAR PARK

Travelling Supporters Information:
Routes: The Ground is situated to the North-East of Cheltenham, 1 mile from the Town Centre off the A46 (Prestbury Road) - Whaddon Road is to the East of the A46 just North of Pittville Circus.

CORBY TOWN FC

Founded: 1948
Former Name(s): Stewarts & Lloyds (1948)
Nickname: 'The Steelmen'
Ground: Rockingham Triangle Stadium, Rockingham Road, Corby, Northants NN17 2AE
Record Attendance: 2,240 (1986)

Colours: Shirts - White
Shorts - Black
Telephone No.: (0536) 401007
Daytime Phone No.: (0536) 522159
Pitch Size: 111 × 74yds
Ground Capacity: 3,000
Seating Capacity: 1,150

GENERAL INFORMATION
Supporters Club Administrator: None
Address: -
Telephone Number: -
Car Parking: At Ground (400 cars)
Coach Parking: At Ground
Nearest Railway Station: Kettering (8 miles)
Nearest Bus Station: Corby (2 miles)
Club Shop: Yes
Opening Times: During Matches
Telephone No.: (0536) 60900
Postal Sales: -
Nearest Police Station: Corby (2 miles)
Police Force: Northamptonshire
Police Telephone No.: (0536) 400400

GROUND INFORMATION
Away Supporters' Entrances: No Segregation
Away Supporters' Sections: -

DISABLED SUPPORTERS INFORMATION
Wheelchairs: Accommodated at front of Stand
Disabled Toilets: Yes
The Blind: No Special Facilities

ADMISSION INFO (1993/94 PRICES)
Adult Standing: £3.50
Adult Seating: £3.50
Child Standing: £2.00
Child Seating: £2.00
Programme Price: 60p
FAX Number: None

CLUBHOUSE
MAIN STAND

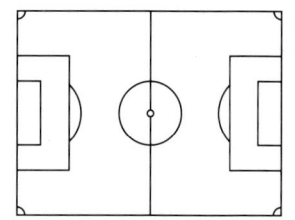

Travelling Supporters Information:
Routes: Exit M1 junction 20 and take the A427 through Market Harborough to Corby. Then take the A6116 towards Rockingham and the ground is situated on the Northern outskirts of the town at the junction of the A6003 and A6116 roads above the Village of Rockingham opposite the entrance to Rockingham Castle Grounds. Entrance is off A6116 Road at Trusthouse Forte Hotel.

CRAWLEY TOWN FC

Founded: 1896
Former Name(s): None
Nickname: 'Red Devils'
Ground: Town Mead, Ifield Avenue, West Green, Crawley, Sussex
Record Attendance: 3,427 (1991)

Colours: Shirts - Red
Shorts - Red
Telephone No.: (0293) 521800
Daytime Phone No.: (0293) 542718
Pitch Size: 110 × 73yds
Ground Capacity: 5,700
Seating Capacity: 250

GENERAL INFORMATION
Supporters Club Administrator: Alain Harper
Address: 33 Nuthurst Close, Ifield, Crawley, Sussex
Telephone Number: (0293) 511764
Car Parking: Car Park at Ground (100 cars)
Coach Parking: Car Park at Ground
Nearest Railway Station: Crawley (0.75 ml)
Nearest Bus Station: By Railway Station
Club Shop: At Ground
Opening Times: Matchdays Only 1.30 - 5.00pm or 6.30 - 9.30pm
Telephone No.: (0293) 542718
Postal Sales: Yes
Nearest Police Station: Kilnmead, Northgate (800 yards)
Police Force: Sussex
Police Telephone No.: (0293) 524242

GROUND INFORMATION
Away Supporters' Entrances: Fire Station End
Away Supporters' Sections: Fire Station End

DISABLED SUPPORTERS INFORMATION
Wheelchairs: Accommodated by arrangement
Disabled Toilets: Available
The Blind: Help available by arrangement

ADMISSION INFO (1993/94 PRICES)
Adult Standing: £4.00
Adult Seating: £4.50
Child Standing: £2.00
Child Seating: £2.00
Programme Price: £1.00
FAX Number: None

Travelling Supporters Information:
Routes: Take M23 to junction 10, A2011 towards Crawley, 3rd exit at roundabout, keeping to the Ring Road. Turn left at the next roundabout into London Road, then second right into Ifield Avenue, ground is next to the fire station.

DORCHESTER TOWN FC

Founded: 1880
Former Name(s): None
Nickname: 'The Magpies'
Ground: The Avenue Stadium, Weymouth Avenue, Dorchester DT1 2RY
Record Attendance: 4,040 (15/10/90)

Colours: Shirts - Black & White Stripes
Shorts - Black
Telephone No.: (0305) 262451/267623
Daytime Phone No.: (0305) 262527
Pitch Size: 110 × 80yds
Ground Capacity: 7,210
Seating Capacity: 710

GENERAL INFORMATION
Supporters Club Administrator: H.G. Gill
Address: 39 Thatcham Pk., Yeovil, Somerset
Telephone Number: (0935) 26029
Car Parking: Car Park at Ground (350 cars)
Coach Parking: At Ground
Nearest Railway Station: Dorchester South & West (both 1 mile)
Nearest Bus Station: Nearby
Club Shop: Yes
Opening Times: During all 1st Team Games
Telephone No.: (0305) 262451
Postal Sales: Yes
Nearest Police Station: Weymouth Avenue, Dorchester
Police Force: Dorset
Police Telephone No.: (0305) 251212

GROUND INFORMATION
Away Supporters' Entrances: Main Stand Side
Away Supporters' Sections: Not Usually Segregated

DISABLED SUPPORTERS INFORMATION
Wheelchairs: Accommodated in Disabled Section
Disabled Toilets: Yes
The Blind: No Special Facilities

ADMISSION INFO (1992/93 PRICES)
Adult Standing: £3.00
Adult Seating: £3.50
Child Standing: £2.00
Child Seating: £2.50
Programme Price: 60p
FAX Number: (0305) 251569

RAILWAY SIDE
OLD GROUND END
WEYMOUTH END
MAIN STAND

Travelling Supporters Information:
Routes: Take Dorchester Bypass (A35) from all directions, ground is on South side of Town adjacent to roundabout at intersection with A354 to Weymouth. Alternatively take Weymouth signs from Town Centre (1.5 miles).

FARNBOROUGH TOWN FC

Founded: 1967
Former Name(s): None
Nickname: 'The Boro'
Ground: John Roberts Ground, Cherrywood Road, Farnborough
Record Attendance: 3,069 (1992)

Colours: Shirts - Yellow with Blue Sleeves
Shorts - Blue
Telephone No.: (0252) 541469
Daytime Phone No.: (0252) 541469
Pitch Size: 115 × 77yds
Ground Capacity: 4,900
Seating Capacity: 500

GENERAL INFORMATION
Supporters Club Administrator: Mark Hardy
Address: 118 Christchurch Drive, Blackwater Camberley, Surrey
Telephone Number: (0276) 35820
Car Parking: Car Park at Ground
Coach Parking: At Ground
Nearest Railway Station: Farnborough (Main), Farnborough North & Frimley
Nearest Bus Station: -
Club Shop: Yes
Opening Times: Matchdays Only
Telephone No.: -
Postal Sales: Via Club
Nearest Police Station: Farnborough
Police Force: Hampshire
Police Telephone No.: (0252) 24545

GROUND INFORMATION
Away Supporters' Entrances: Moor Road
Away Supporters' Sections: Moor Road End

DISABLED SUPPORTERS INFORMATION
Wheelchairs: Accommodated
Disabled Toilets: None
The Blind: No Special Facilities

ADMISSION INFO (1992/93 PRICES)
Adult Standing: £4.00
Adult Seating: £5.00
Child Standing: £2.00
Child Seating: £3.00
Programme Price: £1.00
FAX Number: (0252) 546387

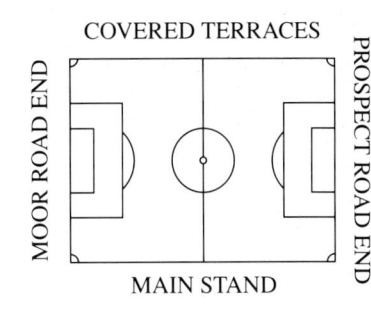

```
           COVERED TERRACES
        ┌─────────────────────┐
M       │                     │  P
O       │                     │  R
O       │                     │  O
R       │                     │  S
        │                     │  P
R       │                     │  E
O       │                     │  C
A       │                     │  T
D       │                     │
        │                     │  R
E       │                     │  O
N       │                     │  A
D       │                     │  D
        │                     │
        │                     │  E
        └─────────────────────┘  N
                                 D
              MAIN STAND
```

Travelling Supporters Information:
Routes: Exit M3 junction 4 heading for Frimley and Farnborough. Take 3rd exit at roundabout A325 Farnborough Road. After R.A.E. Sports Ground turn right into Prospect Avenue then 2nd right into Cherrywood Road. Ground on right.

GLOUCESTER CITY FC

Founded: 1883
Former Name(s): Gloucester YMCA
Nickname: 'The Tigers'
Ground: Meadow Park, Sudmeadow Road, Hempstead, Gloucester   GL2 6HS
Record Attendance: 5,000 (1990)

Colours: Shirts - Yellow
           Shorts - Yellow
Telephone No.: (0452) 523883
Daytime Phone No.: (0452) 523883
Pitch Size: 112 × 72yds
Ground Capacity: 5,000
Seating Capacity: 560

GENERAL INFORMATION
Supporters Club Administrator: J. Lowe
Address: c/o Club
Telephone Number: (0452) 523883
Car Parking: Car Park at Ground (150 cars)
Coach Parking: At Ground
Nearest Railway Station: Gloucester (2 mls)
Nearest Bus Station: Gloucester
Club Shop: Yes
Opening Times: Matchdays Only
Telephone No.: -
Postal Sales: Yes
Nearest Police Station: Gloucester
Police Force: Gloucestershire Constabulary
Police Telephone No.: (0452) 521201

GROUND INFORMATION
Away Supporters' Entrances: Segregation is an option but is normally not used
Away Supporters' Sections: -

DISABLED SUPPORTERS INFORMATION
Wheelchairs: Accommodated by Arrangement
Disabled Toilets: Two Available
The Blind: No Special Facilities

ADMISSION INFO (1993/94 PRICES)
Adult Standing: £3.00
Adult Seating: £4.00
Child Standing: £1.00
Child Seating: £2.00
Programme Price: 80p
FAX Number: (0452) 301330

```
              MAIN STAND
        ┌─────────────────────┐
   O    │                     │   O
   P    │                     │   P
   E    │                     │   E
   N    │                     │   N
        │                     │
   T    │                     │   T
   E    │                     │   E
   R    │                     │   R
   R    │                     │   R
   A    │                     │   A
   C    │                     │   C
   E    │                     │   E
        └─────────────────────┘
           COVERED TERRACE
```

Travelling Supporters Information:
Routes: Take A40 into the City Centre towards historic docks, then Severn Road, right into Hempstead Lane and right again into Sudmeadow Road. Ground 50 yards on left.

GRESLEY ROVERS FC

Founded: 1882
Former Name(s): None
Nickname: 'The Moatmen'
Ground: The Moat Ground, Moat Street, Church Gresley, Swadlincote, Derbyshire
Record Attendance: 3,950 (1957-58)

Colours: Shirts - Red with White Sleeves
Shorts - Red
Telephone No.: (0283) 216315
Daytime Phone No.: (0283) 221881
Pitch Size: 110 × 70yds
Ground Capacity: 2,500
Seating Capacity: 415

GENERAL INFORMATION
Supporters Club Administrator: Nick Holmshaw
Address: 67 Castle Road, Castle Gresley, Swadlincote, Derbyshire
Telephone Number: (0283) 218530
Car Parking: At Ground
Coach Parking: At Ground
Nearest Railway Station: Burton-on-Trent (5 miles)
Nearest Bus Station: Swadlincote (1 mile)
Club Shop: Yes
Opening Times: Matchdays Only
Telephone No.: (0283) 216315
Postal Sales: Yes
Nearest Police Station: Swadlincote
Police Force: Derbyshire
Police Telephone No.: (0283) 550101

GROUND INFORMATION
Away Supporters' Entrances: Derby Road
Away Supporters' Sections: Derby Road

DISABLED SUPPORTERS INFORMATION
Wheelchairs: Accommodated
Disabled Toilets: None
The Blind: No Special Facilities

ADMISSION INFO (1993/94 PRICES)
Adult Standing: £3.50
Adult Seating: £3.50
Child Standing: £1.75
Child Seating: £1.75
Programme Price: 70p
FAX Number: None

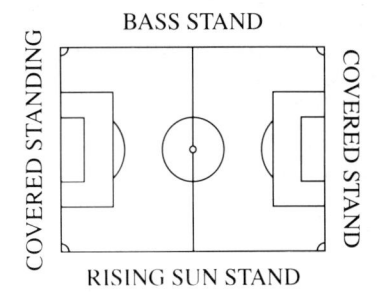

BASS STAND
COVERED STANDING
COVERED STAND
RISING SUN STAND

Travelling Supporters Information:
Routes: Take the M42 to A444 Burton-on-Trent exit and head for Castle Gresley. In Castle Gresley turn right onto the A514 (signposted Derby). Turn right at the top of the hill (Miners Arms) then first left into Church Street. Take 2nd exit on the left (School Street) and Moat Street is next left.

HALESOWEN TOWN FC

Founded: 1873
Former Name(s): None
Nickname: 'The Yeltz'
Ground: The Grove, Old Hawne Lane, Halesowen, West Midlands
Record Attendance: 5,000 (19/11/55)
Colours: Shirts - Blue
Shorts - White
Telephone No.: (021) 550-2179
Daytime Phone No.: (021) 550-2179
Pitch Size: 110 × 71yds
Ground Capacity: 5,000
Seating Capacity: 420

GENERAL INFORMATION
Supporters Club Administrator: Paul Flood
Address: 112 Blackberry Lane, Halesowen
Telephone Number: (021) 550-8999
Car Parking: Room for 70 Cars at Ground
Coach Parking: Available near Ground
Nearest Railway Station: Old Hill (2 miles)
Nearest Bus Station: On main Stourbridge Road.
Club Shop: Yes
Opening Times: Matchdays Only
Telephone No.: (021) 550-2179
Postal Sales: Yes
Nearest Police Station: Halesowen
Police Force: West Midlands
Police Telephone No.: (021) 626-8030

GROUND INFORMATION
Away Supporters' Entrances: No Segregation
Away Supporters' Sections: No Segregation

DISABLED SUPPORTERS INFORMATION
Wheelchairs: Accommodated
Disabled Toilets: None
The Blind: No Special Facilities

ADMISSION INFO (1992/93 PRICES)
Adult Standing: £3.00
Adult Seating: £3.50
Child Standing: £1.50
Child Seating: £2.00
Programme Price: 60p
FAX Number: -

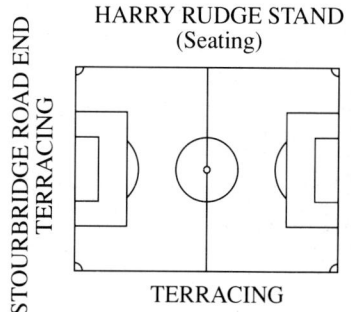

HARRY RUDGE STAND (Seating)
STOURBRIDGE ROAD END TERRACING
OLD HAWNE LANE END COVERED TERRACING
TERRACING

Travelling Supporters Information:
Routes: Exit M5 at junction 3, follow A456 towards Kidderminster to 1st Island and turn right at the signpost onto the A458 towards Dudley. Turn left at the next island and follow the signpost onto A458 towards Stourbridge. At the next island take the 3rd exit, the ground is approximately 400 yards on the left.

HASTINGS TOWN FC

Founded: 1895
Former Name(s): Hastings & St. Leonards Amateurs
Nickname: 'The Town'
Ground: The Pilot Field, Elphinstone Road, Hastings   TN34 2AX
Record Attendance: 2,248 (1992/93)

Colours: Shirts - White with Red Trim
   Shorts - White with Red Trim
Telephone No.: (0424) 444635/430517
Daytime Phone No.: (0424) 444635
Pitch Size: 110 × 78yds
Ground Capacity: 10,000
Seating Capacity: 900

GENERAL INFORMATION
Supporters Club Administrator: R. Wolfe
Address: 32 Abbotsfield Close, Hastings
Telephone Number: (0424) 427349
Car Parking: Street Parking
Coach Parking: Street Parking
Nearest Railway Station: Hastings (1.5 mls)
Nearest Bus Station: Town Centre (1.5 miles)
Club Shop: Yes
Opening Times: Match Days Only
Telephone No.: (0424) 430517
Postal Sales: via R. Baker, 35 Edlescombe Road North, St. Leonards-on-Sea
Nearest Police Station: Hastings
Police Force: East Sussex
Police Telephone No.: (0424) 425000

GROUND INFORMATION
Away Supporters' Entrances: No Segregation
Away Supporters' Sections: No Segregation

DISABLED SUPPORTERS INFORMATION
Wheelchairs: Accommodated by arrangement
Disabled Toilets: None
The Blind: No Special Facilities

ADMISSION INFO (1993/94 PRICES)
Adult Standing: £3.50
Adult Seating: £4.50
Child Standing: £2.00
Child Seating: £2.50
Programme Price: 80p
FAX Number: None

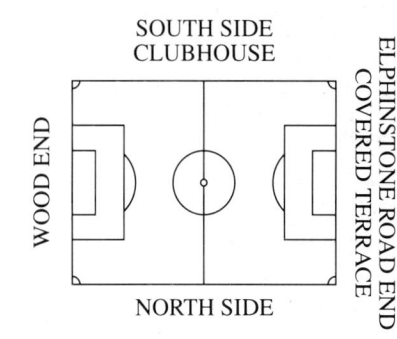

SOUTH SIDE
CLUBHOUSE

WOOD END

ELPHINSTONE ROAD END
COVERED TERRACE

NORTH SIDE

Travelling Supporters Information:
Routes: From A21 turn left into St. Helens Road (A2101). After 1 mile turn left into St. Helens Park Road which leads into Downs Road. Follow Downs Road to the end then turn left at the T-junction. Ground is on the right.

HEDNESFORD TOWN FC

Founded: 1880
Former Name(s): Club formed by amalgamation of West Hill & Hill Top in 1880
Nickname: 'The Pitmen'
Ground: Cross Keys Ground, Hill Street, Hednesford
Record Attendance: 10,000 (1919-20)

Colours: Shirts - White & Black
Shorts - Black
Telephone No.: (0543) 422870
Daytime Phone No.: (0543) 422870
Pitch Size: 114 × 70yds
Ground Capacity: 3,500
Seating Capacity: 500

GENERAL INFORMATION
Supporters Club Administrator: Phil Lloyd
Address: c/o Club
Telephone Number: -
Car Parking: Space for 200 cars at ground
Coach Parking: Available at ground
Nearest Railway Station: Hednesford (0.5m)
Nearest Bus Station: Hednesford
Club Shop: Yes
Opening Times: Home matches only
Telephone No.: (0543) 422870
Postal Sales: Yes
Nearest Police Station: Hednesford
Police Force: Staffordshire
Police Telephone No.: (0543) 574545

GROUND INFORMATION
Away Supporters' Entrances: No Segregation
Away Supporters' Sections: No Segregation

DISABLED SUPPORTERS INFORMATION
Wheelchairs: Accommodated
Disabled Toilets: None
The Blind: Please contact club for further information

ADMISSION INFO (1993/94 PRICES)
Adult Standing: £3.20
Adult Seating: £3.20
Child Standing: £1.60
Child Seating: £1.60
Programme Price: 80p
FAX Number: None

HEATH HAYES

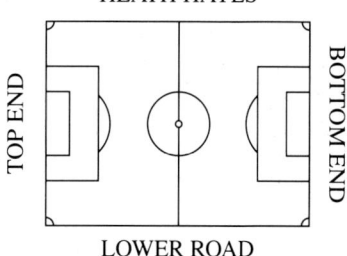

TOP END

BOTTOM END

LOWER ROAD

Travelling Supporters Information:
Routes: Exit M6 at junction 11 to Cannock and follow A460 towards Hednesford. After 2 miles turn right opposite the Shell Garage, ground is at bottom of hill on right.

MOOR GREEN FC

Founded: 1901
Former Name(s): None
Nickname: 'The Moors'
Ground: The Moorlands, Sherwood Road, Hall Green, Birmingham B28 0EX
Record Attendance: 5,000 (1951)

Colours: Shirts - Sky Blue
Shorts - Royal Blue
Telephone No.: (021) 624-2727
Daytime Phone No.: (021) 743-0991
Pitch Size: 116 × 73yds
Ground Capacity: 3,250
Seating Capacity: 250

GENERAL INFORMATION
Supporters Club Administrator: Julie Allen
Address: 54 Acheson Road, Hall Green, Birmingham B28 0TS
Telephone Number: (021) 745-3308
Car Parking: 150 Cars at Ground
Coach Parking: At Ground
Nearest Railway Station: Hall Green/Yardley Wood (0.5 mile)
Nearest Bus Station: Digbeth
Club Shop: Yes
Opening Times: Matchdays Only (30 mins before & after the Game)
Telephone No.: (021) 624-2727
Postal Sales: Yes
Nearest Police Station: Acocks Green
Police Force: West Midlands
Police Telephone No.: (021) 706-8111

GROUND INFORMATION
Away Supporters' Entrances: Sherwood Road
Away Supporters' Sections: No Segregation

DISABLED SUPPORTERS INFORMATION
Wheelchairs: Accommodated
Disabled Toilets: None
The Blind: By Arrangement

ADMISSION INFO (1993/94 PRICES)
Adult Standing: £3.00
Adult Seating: £3.50
Child Standing: £1.50
Child Seating: £2.00
Programme Price: 60p
FAX Number: -

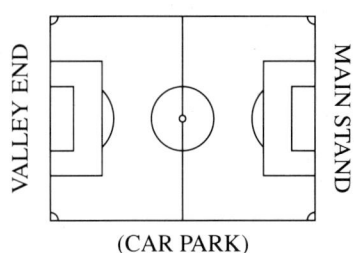

```
          SCHOOL SIDE
   ┌─────────────────────┐
V  │                     │  M
A  │                     │  A
L  │                     │  I
L  │          ○          │  N
E  │                     │
Y  │                     │  S
   │                     │  T
E  │                     │  A
N  │                     │  N
D  │                     │  D
   └─────────────────────┘
        (CAR PARK)
       SHERWOOD ROAD
```

Travelling Supporters Information:
Routes: Exit M42 at Junction 4, joining A34. Travel towards Birmingham City Centre for 4 miles until Highfield Road in Hall Green, South Birmingham. Sherwood Road is 2nd right off Highfield Road.

NUNEATON BOROUGH FC

Founded: 1937 (Re-formed 1991)
Former Name(s): Nuneaton Town FC
Nickname: 'The Borough'
Ground: Manor Park, Beaumont Road, Nuneaton, Warks   CV11 5HD
Record Attendance: 22,114 vs Rotherham (1967)

Colours: Shirts - Blue & White Stripes
            Shorts - Blue
Telephone No.: (0203) 385738
Daytime Phone No.: (0203) 374043
Pitch Size: 110 × 72yds
Ground Capacity: 6,000
Seating Capacity: 600

GENERAL INFORMATION
Supporters Club Administrator: John Tallis
Address: c/o Club
Telephone Number: (0203) 392112
Car Parking: At Ground
Coach Parking: At Ground
Nearest Railway Station: Nuneaton Trent Valley (1 mile)
Nearest Bus Station: Nuneaton (1 mile)
Club Shop: Yes - The Boro Shop, 35 Clarence Street, Nuneaton
Opening Times: Matchdays
Telephone No.: (0203) 374043
Postal Sales: Yes
Nearest Police Station: Nuneaton
Police Force: Warwickshire
Police Telephone No.: (0203) 641111

GROUND INFORMATION
Away Supporters' Entrances: Top Cock & Bear Bridge
Away Supporters' Sections: Canal Side

DISABLED SUPPORTERS INFORMATION
Wheelchairs: Accommodated
Disabled Toilets: At rear of Main Stand
The Blind: Anker Radio Hospital Commentary

ADMISSION INFO (1993/94 PRICES)
Adult Standing: £3.00
Adult Seating: £4.00
Child Standing: £1.30
Child Seating: £1.80
Programme Price: 60p
FAX Number: None

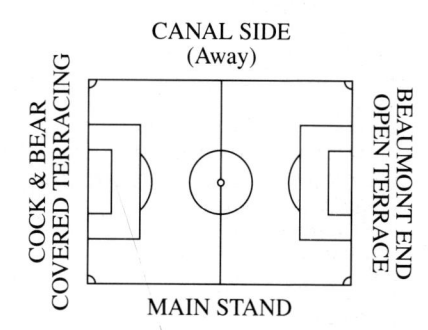

Travelling Supporters Information:
Routes: Exit M6 junction 3 and take A444 to Nuneaton. At roundabout by hospital turn left into College Street to the Bull Ring. Turn right into Greenmoor Road and follow to end (approximately 0.75 mile) turn right and cross over bridge and ground is on left.

SITTINGBOURNE FC

Founded: 1881
Former Name(s): Sittingbourne United FC
Nickname: 'The Brickies', 'The Bourne'
Ground: Central Park Eurolink, Sittingbourne, Kent   ME10 3SB
Record Attendance: 5,583 vs Gravesend (1961)
Colours: Shirts - Red   Shorts - Black
Telephone No.: (0795) 475547
Daytime Phone No.: (0795) 474053
Pitch Size: 110 × 72yds
Ground Capacity: 3,200
Seating Capacity: 400

GENERAL INFORMATION
Supporters Club Administrator: Ann Morrison
Address: c/o Club
Telephone Number: -
Car Parking: At Ground
Coach Parking: At Ground
Nearest Railway Station: Sittingbourne (0.75 mile)
Nearest Bus Station: Sittingbourne
Club Shop: Yes
Opening Times: Daily
Telephone No.: (0795) 475547
Postal Sales: Yes
Nearest Police Station: Sittingbourne
Police Force: Kent Constabulary
Police Telephone No.: (0795) 477055

GROUND INFORMATION
Away Supporters' Entrances: No Segregation
Away Supporters' Sections: No Segregation

DISABLED SUPPORTERS INFORMATION
Wheelchairs: Accommodated
Disabled Toilets: Yes - Near Social Club
The Blind: No Special Facilities

ADMISSION INFO   (1993/94 PRICES)
Adult Standing: £3.00
Adult Seating: £4.00
Child Standing: £2.00
Child Seating: £3.00
Programme Price: £1.00
FAX Number: (0795) 430776

MAIN STAND
OPEN TERRACING
OPEN TERRACING
COVERED STANDING

Travelling Supporters Information:
Routes: Take A2 into Sittingbourne Town Centre and follow one-way system into St. Michaels Road, then follow signs for ground.

SOLIHULL BOROUGH FC

Founded: 1951
Former Name(s): Lincoln FC
Nickname: 'The Boro'
Ground: The Moorlands, Sherwood Road, Hall Green, Birmingham   B28 0EX
Record Attendance: 1,260 (1993)

Colours: Shirts - Red
           Shorts - White
Telephone No.: (021) 745-6758
Daytime Phone No.: (021) 745-6758
Pitch Size: 116 × 73yds
Ground Capacity: 3,000
Seating Capacity: 244

GENERAL INFORMATION
Supporters Club Administrator: Ian Marks
Address: 10 Tylers Grove, Monkpath, Solihull   B90 4TJ
Telephone Number: (021) 745-6758
Car Parking: 150 Cars at Ground
Coach Parking: At Ground
Nearest Railway Station: Hall Green/Yardley Wood (0.5 mile)
Nearest Bus Station: Digbeth
Club Shop: Yes
Opening Times: Matchdays Only
Telephone No.: (021) 745-6758
Postal Sales: Yes
Nearest Police Station: Acocks Green
Police Force: West Midlands
Police Telephone No.: (021) 706-8111

Note : Solihull Borough are ground-sharing with Moor Green FC.

GROUND INFORMATION
Away Supporters' Entrances: Sherwood Road
Away Supporters' Sections: No Segregation

DISABLED SUPPORTERS INFORMATION
Wheelchairs: Accommodated
Disabled Toilets: None
The Blind: By Arrangement

ADMISSION INFO (1993/94 PRICES)
Adult Standing: £3.00
Adult Seating: £3.50
Child Standing: £1.00
Child Seating: £1.50
Programme Price: 60p
FAX Number: (021) 744-9351

```
              SCHOOL SIDE

  V                                    M
  A                                    A
  L                                    I
  L                                    N
  E                                    
  Y                                    S
                                       T
  E                                    A
  N                                    N
  D                                    D

              (CAR PARK)
            SHERWOOD ROAD
```

Travelling Supporters Information:
Routes: Exit M42 at Junction 4, joining A34. Approximately 4 miles to Birmingham City Centre then a further 4 miles until Highfield Road in Hall Green, South Birmingham. Take 2nd right into Sherwood Road for the ground.

TROWBRIDGE TOWN FC

Founded: 1880
Former Name(s): None
Nickname: 'The Bees'
Ground: Frome Road, Trowbridge, Wiltshire
Record Attendance: 9,009 vs Weymouth

Colours: Shirts - Old Gold
Shorts - Black
Telephone No.: (0225) 752076
Daytime Phone No.: (0225) 467336
Pitch Size: 120 × 75yds
Ground Capacity: 5,000
Seating Capacity: 200

GENERAL INFORMATION
Supporters Club Administrator: J. Irons
Address: c/o Club
Telephone Number: (0225) 752076
Car Parking: 200 Cars at Ground
Coach Parking: 2 at Ground
Nearest Railway Station: Trowbridge (0.75 mile)
Nearest Bus Station: Trowbridge
Club Shop: Yes
Opening Times: Match Days Only
Telephone No.: (0225) 752076
Postal Sales: Yes
Nearest Police Station: Trowbridge
Police Force: Wiltshire
Police Telephone No.: (0225) 763101

Photo - A. Meaden

GROUND INFORMATION
Away Supporters' Entrances: No Segregation
Away Supporters' Sections: No Segregation

DISABLED SUPPORTERS INFORMATION
Wheelchairs: Accommodated
Disabled Toilets: None
The Blind: No Special Facilities

ADMISSION INFO (1993/94 PRICES)
Adult Standing: £3.50
Adult Seating: £4.00
Child Standing: £2.00
Child Seating: £2.50
Programme Price: 60p
FAX Number: (0225) 766953   c/o Presto Print

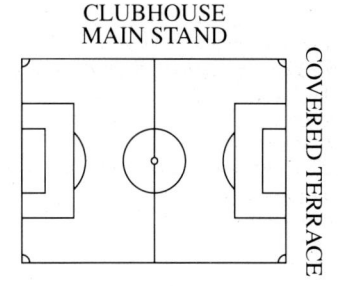

```
       CLUBHOUSE
       MAIN STAND        COVERED TERRACE
```

Travelling Supporters Information:
Routes: Take A361 to Trowbridge and on entering the Town, follow Ring Road signs to Frome. Ground situated in Frome Road 100 yards on left past The Ship Inn Public House - Entrance marked.

WATERLOOVILLE FC

Founded: 1905
Former Name(s): None
Nickname: 'The Ville'
Ground: Jubilee Park, Ashton Road, Waterlooville, Hants.
Record Attendance: 4,500 (1976/77)

Colours: Shirts - White
Shorts - Navy Blue
Telephone No.: (0705) 263867/230114
Daytime Phone No.: (0705) 257411
Pitch Size: 110 × 70yds
Ground Capacity: 5,000
Seating Capacity: 500

GENERAL INFORMATION
Supporters Club Administrator: E. Hadden
Address: 36 Winchfield Crescent, Bedhampton, Hants.
Telephone Number: (0705) 476092
Car Parking: Space for 300 Cars at Ground
Coach Parking: At Ground
Nearest Railway Station: Havant/Cosham (4 miles)
Nearest Bus Station: Town Centre (0.5 mile)
Club Shop: Yes
Opening Times: Matchdays Only
Telephone No.: (0705) 263867
Postal Sales: Yes
Nearest Police Station: Cowplain
Police Force: Hampshire
Police Telephone No.: (0705) 321111

GROUND INFORMATION
Away Supporters' Entrances: Car Park End
Away Supporters' Sections: No usual segregation

DISABLED SUPPORTERS INFORMATION
Wheelchairs: Accommodated
Disabled Toilets: Yes
The Blind: No Special Facilities

ADMISSION INFO (1992/93 PRICES)
Adult Standing: £3.00
Adult Seating: £3.50
Child Standing: £1.50
Child Seating: £2.00
Programme Price: 60p
FAX Number: -

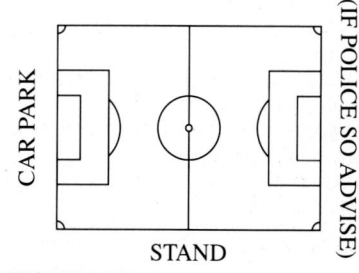

Travelling Supporters Information:
Routes: From London or the North take A3(M) until the signpost to Waterlooville. Turn off and proceed straight across the 1st Roundabout. Turn left at the next roundabout and take the right exit off the following roundabout on the Hambledon Road. At the next roundabout, go fully around, and return towards Waterlooville. The first turning on the left is Ashton Road and the ground is on the industrial estate nearby.

WORCESTER CITY FC

Founded: 1902
Former Name(s): Berwick Rangers
Nickname: 'The City'
Ground: St.Georges Lane, Worcester WR1 1QT
Record Attendance: 17,042 (1958/59)

Colours: Shirts - Blue & White Quarters
Shorts - Blue
Telephone No.: (0905) 23003
Daytime Phone No.: (0905) 23003
Pitch Size: 110 × 73yds
Ground Capacity: 10,000
Seating Capacity: 1,500

GENERAL INFORMATION
Supporters Club Administrator: Malcolm Smith
Address: 64 Hallow Road, Worcester WR2 6BY
Telephone Number: (0905) 422905
Car Parking: Street Parking
Coach Parking: Street Parking
Nearest Railway Station: Foregate Street/Shrub Hill
Nearest Bus Station: Crowngate Bus Station
Club Shop: At Ground
Opening Times: Matchdays (45 mins before kick-off and during game)
Telephone No.: (0905) 20660
Postal Sales: Contact : John Hawkins, 44 Bromsgrove Street, Barbourne, Worcester
Nearest Police Station: Deansway
Police Force: West Mercia Constabulary
Police Telephone No.: (0905) 723888

GROUND INFORMATION
Away Supporters' Entrances: When segregation - turnstile at Canal End
Away Supporters' Sections: Canal End

DISABLED SUPPORTERS INFORMATION
Wheelchairs: Accommodated by Arrangement
Disabled Toilets: None
The Blind: No Special Facilities

ADMISSION INFO (1993/94 PRICES)
Adult Standing: £3.50
Adult Seating: £4.10
Child Standing: £1.80
Child Seating: £2.05
Programme Price: 70p
FAX Number: (0905) 26668

BROOKSIDE
BROOKSIDE
CANAL END
MAIN STAND

Travelling Supporters Information:
Routes: From North & East: Exit M5 junction 5 and follow A38 through Droitwich into Worcester. Take a left turn 500 yards after 1st set of traffic lights (signposted); From South & West: Exit M5 junction 7 and follow A44 into Worcester, go past Racecourse and follow A38 towards Bromsgrove. Right turn signposted.

BEAZER HOMES MIDLAND DIVISION

ARMITAGE '90' FC
Founded: 1990 **Ground**: Rugeley Road, Kings Bromley, Burton-on-Trent, DE15 7JG. **Ground Capacity**: 1,500 **Seating Capacity**: 300. **Tel. No**: (0543) 491077

BEDWORTH UNITED FC
Founded: 1896 **Nickname**: 'The Greenbacks' **Former Name**: Bedworth Town FC **Ground**: The Oval, Coventry Road, Bedworth Warwickshire. **Ground Capacity**: 10,000 **Seating Capacity**: 300. **Tel. No**: (0203) 314302

BILSTON TOWN FC
Founded: 1895 **Nickname**: 'Borough' 'Steelmen' **Former Names**: Bilston United FC, Bilston FC. **Ground**: Queen Street, Bilston, West Midlands. **Ground Capacity**: 5,000 **Seating Capacity**: 450. **Tel. No**: (0902) 491498; (0902) 491799 (Secretary)

BRIDGNORTH TOWN FC
Founded: 1946 **Nickname**: 'The Town' **Former Name**: St. Leonards Old Boys FC. **Ground**: Crown Meadow, Innage Lane, Bridgnorth, Shropshire. **Ground Capacity**: 2,000 **Seating Capacity**: 250. **Tel. No**: (0746) 762747

CLEVEDON TOWN FC
Founded: 1880 **Ground**: The Hand Stadium, Davis Lane, Clevedon, Avon. **Ground Capacity**: 3,650 **Seating Capacity**: 300. **Tel. No**: (0275) 871636

DUDLEY TOWN FC
Founded: 1883 **Nickname**: 'The Robins' **Ground**: Round Oak Stadium, John Street, Brierley Hill, West Midlands. **Ground Capacity**: 3,000 **Seating Capacity**: 230. **Tel. No**: (0922) 475541

EVESHAM UNITED FC
Founded: 1945 **Nickname**: 'The Robins' **Former Name**: Evesham Town FC. **Ground**: Common Road, Evesham, Worcs. WR11 4PU. **Ground Capacity**: 2,500 **Seating Capacity**: 350. **Tel. No**: (0386) 442303

FOREST GREEN ROVERS FC
Founded: 1889 **Nickname**: 'The Green' 'The Rovers' **Former Name**: Stroud FC. **Ground**: The Lawn, Nympsfield Road, Forest Green, Nailsworth, Stroud, Glos. **Total Capacity**: 4,500 **Seating**: 200. **Tel. No**: (0453) 834890

GRANTHAM TOWN FC
Founded: 1874 **Nickname**: 'Gingerbreads' **Ground**: South Kesteven Stadium, Trent Road, Grantham, Lincs. **Ground Capacity**: 7,000 **Seating Capacity**: 750. **Tel. No**: (0476) 62011; (0476) 64408 (Secretary)

HINCKLEY TOWN FC
Founded: 1958 **Nickname**: 'Eagles' **Former Name**: Westfield Rovers FC. **Ground**: Leicester Road, Hinckley, Leicester. **Ground Capacity**: 3,000 **Seating Capacity**: 250. **Tel. No**: (0455) 615062

KINGS LYNN FC
Founded: 1879 **Nickname**: 'The Linnetts' **Ground**: The Walks Stadium, Tennyson Road, Kings Lynn. **Ground Capacity**: 7,500 **Seating Capacity**: 1,200. **Tel. No**: (0733) 267272 (Secretary's Home)

LEICESTER UNITED FC
Founded: 1900 **Nickname**: 'United' **Former Name**: Enderby Town FC. **Ground**: United Park, Winchester Road, Blaby, Leicester LE8 3HN. **Ground Capacity**: 4,000 **Seating Capacity**: 228. **Tel. No**: (0533) 882358

NEWPORT AFC
Founded: 1989 **Nickname**: 'The Exiles' **Ground**: Sharing with Gloucester City at Meadow Park, Sudmeadow Road, Hempstead, Gloucester. **Ground Capacity**: 5,000 **Seating Capacity**: 560. **Tel. No**: (0633) 280932 (Sec)

RACING CLUB WARWICK FC
Founded: 1919 **Nickname**: 'Racing' **Former Name**: Saltisford Rovers FC. **Ground**: Townend Meadow, Hampton Road, Warwick. **Ground Capacity**: 1,000 **Seating Capacity**: 200. **Tel. No**: (0926) 612675 (Sec)

REDDITCH UNITED FC
Founded: 1892 **Nickname**: 'The Reds' **Ground**: Valley Stadium, Bromsgrove Road, Redditch. **Ground Capacity**: 7,000 **Seating Capacity**: 250. **Tel. No**: (0527) 26603 (Secretary)

RUSHDEN & DIAMONDS FC
Founded: 1890 **Nickname**: 'The Russians' **Former Name**: Rushden Town FC & Irthlingborough Diamonds FC. **Ground**: Nene Park, Irthlingborough, Northants. **Capacity**: 5,000 **Seating**: 2,000 **Tel. No**: (0933) 57968

STOURBRIDGE FC
Founded: 1876 **Nickname**: 'The Glassboys' **Former Name**: Stourbridge Standard FC. **Ground**: War Memorial Athletic Ground, High Street, Amblecote, Stourbridge DY8 4EB. **Ground Capacity**: 2,000 **Seating Capacity**: 260. **Tel. No**: (0384) 392975 (Secretary)

SUTTON COLDFIELD TOWN FC
Founded: 1879 **Nickname**: 'The Royals' **Former Name**: Sutton Town FC. **Ground**: Central Ground, Coles Lane, Sutton Coldfield, West Midlands B72 1NL. **Capacity**: 2,000 **Seating**: 200 **Tel**: (021) 354-2997

TAMWORTH FC *
Founded: 1933 **Nickname**: 'The Lambs' ' The Town' **Ground**: The Lamb Ground, Kettlebrook, Tamworth B79 1HA. **Ground Capacity**: 2,500 **Seating Capacity**: 400. **Tel. No**: (0827) 65798; (0827) 66786 (Secretary)

V.S. RUGBY FC
Founded: 1956 **Former Names**: Valley Sports FC, Valley Sports Rugby FC. **Ground**: Butlin Road, Rugby, Warks. CV21 3ST. **Capacity**: 6,000 **Seating**: 216 **Tel.**: (0788) 543692   * Club in Receivership

WESTON-SUPER-MARE AFC
Founded: 1948 **Nickname**: 'The Seagulls' **Ground**: Woodspring Park, Winterstoke Road, Weston-Super-Mare, Avon, BS23 2YG. **Ground Capacity**: 4,000. **Seating Capacity**: 250. **Tel. No**: (0934) 621618

YATE TOWN FC
Founded: Reformed 1946 **Nickname**: 'The Bluebells' **Former Name**: Yate YMCA FC, Yate Rovers FC. **Ground**: Lodge Road, Yate, Bristol, BS17 5LE. **Ground Capacity**: 2,000. **Seating**: 226. **Tel. No**: (0454) 228103

BEAZER HOMES SOUTHERN DIVISION

ASHFORD TOWN FC
Founded: 1930 **Nickname**: 'Nuts & Bolts' **Ground**: The Homelands, Ashford Road, Kingsnorth, Ashford, Kent TN26 1NT. **Ground Capacity**: 3,000 **Seating Capacity**: 495. **Tel. No**: (0233) 611838 (Ground)

BALDOCK TOWN FC
Founded: 1889 **Nickname**: 'Reds' **Ground**: Norton Road, Baldock, Herts SG7 5AU. **Ground Capacity**: 3,000 **Seating Capacity**: 200. **Tel. No**: (0462) 436647

BRAINTREE TOWN FC
Founded: 1894 **Nickname**: 'The Iron' **Former Names**: Manor Works FC, Crittall Athletic FC, Braintree & Crittall Athletic FC, Braintree FC, Braintree Town FC. **Ground**: Cressing Road Stadium, Clockhouse Way, Cressing Road, Braintree, Essex. **Ground Capacity**: 4,000 **Seating Capacity**: 240. **Tel. No**: (0376) 326234

BUCKINGHAM TOWN FC
Founded: 1883 **Nickname**: 'The Robins' **Ground**: Ford Meadow, Ford Street, Buckingham, Bucks. **Ground Capacity**: 4,000 **Seating Capacity**: 100. **Tel. No**: (0280) 816257; (0280) 822800 (Secretary)

BURNHAM FC
Founded: 1878 **Nickname**: 'The Blues' **Former Name**: Burnham & Hillingdon FC. **Ground**: Wymers Wood Road, Burnham, Slough, SL1 8JG. **Ground Capacity**: 2,000 **Seating Capacity**: 224. **Tel. No**: (0628) 602697; (0628) 660265 (Secretary)

BURY TOWN FC
Founded: 1872 **Nickname**: 'Blues' **Former Name**: Bury United FC. **Ground**: Ram Meadow, Cotton Lane, Bury St. Edmunds, Suffolk. **Ground Capacity**: 3,500 **Seating Capacity**: 300. **Tel. No**: (0284) 810679 (Sec)

CANTERBURY CITY FC
Founded: 1947. **Nickname**: 'City'. **Former Name**: Canterbury Waverley FC. **Ground**: Kingsmead Stadium, Kingsmead Road, Canterbury, Kent. **Ground Capacity**: 5,000 **Seating Capacity**: 200. **Tel. No**: (0227) 762220

DUNSTABLE FC
Founded: 1965 **Nickname**: 'The Blues' **Former Name**: Dunstable Town FC. **Ground**: Creasy Park, Creasy Park Road, Dunstable, Beds. **Ground Capacity**: 6,000 **Seating Capacity**: 400. **Tel. No**: (0582) 606691

ERITH & BELVEDERE FC
Founded: 1908 **Nickname**: 'The Dere's' **Ground**: Park View, Lower Road, Belvedere, Kent. **Ground Capacity**: 1,500 **Seating Capacity**: 250. **Tel. No**: (081) 311-0650

FAREHAM TOWN FC
Founded: 1947 **Nickname**: 'The Town' **Ground**: Cams Alders Stadium, Highfield Avenue, Fareham, Hants, PO14 1JA. **Ground Capacity**: 3,500 **Seating Capacity**: 450. **Tel. No**: (0329) 231151; (0329) 285432 (Secretary)

FISHER ATHLETIC FC
Founded: 1908 **Nickname**: 'The Fish' **Ground**: Surrey Docks Stadium, Salter Road, London, SE16 1LQ. **Ground Capacity**: 5,700 **Seating Capacity**: 600. **Tel. No**: (071) 231-5144

GRAVESEND & NORTHFLEET FC
Founded: 1946 **Nickname**: 'The Fleet' **Former Names**: Formed by the amalgamation of Gravesend United FC & Northfleet United FC. **Ground**: Stonebridge Road, Northfleet, Gravesend, Kent. **Ground Capacity**: 9,900 **Seating Capacity**: 800. **Tel. No**: (0474) 533796

HAVANT TOWN FC
Founded: 1898 **Nickname**: 'Town' **Former Names**: Havant Rovers FC, Havant & Leigh Park FC. **Ground**: Westleigh Park, Martins Road, Havant, Hants. **Ground Capacity**: 6,000 **Seating Capacity**: 240. **Tel. No**: (0705) 267276 (Secretary)

MARGATE FC
Founded: 1896 **Nickname**: 'The Gate' **Former Name**: Thanet United FC. **Ground**: Hartsdown Park, Hartsdown Road, Margate. **Ground Capacity**: 6,000 **Seating Capacity**: 350. **Tel. No**: (0843) 291040

NEWPORT I.O.W. FC
Founded: 1888 **Nickname**: 'The Port' **Ground**: St. George's Park, St. George's Way, Newport, I.O.W. **Ground Capacity**: 5,000 **Seating Capacity**: 300. **Tel. No**: (0983) 525027

POOLE TOWN FC
Founded: 1880 **Nickname**: 'The Dolphins' **Ground**: Poole Stadium, Wimborne Road, Poole, Dorset, BH15 2BP. **Ground Capacity**: 6,500 **Seating Capacity**: 1,400. **Tel. No**: (0202) 536906 (Secretary)

SALISBURY FC
Founded: 1947 **Nickname**: 'The Whites' **Former Names**: Salisbury Corinthian FC, Salisbury City FC. **Ground**: Victoria Park, Castle Road, Salisbury. **Ground Capacity**: 4,000 **Seating Capacity**: 320. **Tel. No**: (0722) 326454 (Secretary)

SUDBURY TOWN FC
Founded: 1898 **Nickname**: 'The Boro' **Ground**: Priory Stadium, Priory Walk, Sudbury, Suffolk. **Ground Capacity**: 5,000 **Seating Capacity**: 300. **Tel. No**: (0787) 379095

TONBRIDGE AFC
Founded: 1948 **Ground**: Longmead Stadium, Darenth Avenue, Tonbridge, Kent. **Ground Capacity**: 5,000 **Seating Capacity**: 200 **Tel. No**: (0732) 352417

WEALDSTONE FC
Founded: 1899 **Nickname**: 'Stones' 'Royals' **Ground**: Vicarage Road Stadium, Watford. **Ground Capacity**: 23,000 **Seating Capacity**: 10,158 **Tel**: (0923) 212916

WEYMOUTH FC
Founded: 1890 **Nickname**: 'The Terriers' **Ground**: Wessex Stadium, Radipole Lane, Weymouth, Dorset. **Ground Capacity**: 9,999 **Seating Capacity**: 850. **Tel. No**: (0305) 785558

WITNEY TOWN FC
Founded: 1885 **Nickname**: 'Town' **Ground**: Oakley Park, Downs Road, Witney, Oxon, OX8 5LY. **Ground Capacity**: 3,500 **Seating Capacity**: 234. **Tel. No**: (0993) 702549

GM Vauxhall Conf. Season 1992/93

	ALT	BAT	BOS	BRO	DAG	FAR	GAT	KET	KID	MAC	MER	NOR	RUN	SLO	STA	STC	TEL	WEL	WIT	WOK	WYC	YEO
Altrincham	■	1-0	1-1	2-2	1-0	2-2	0-1	3-0	2-2	1-0	0-1	0-0	0-2	1-1	1-5	0-0	0-3	2-0	2-1	1-0	0-2	1-2
Bath City	3-0	■	2-1	0-3	2-1	5-2	1-1	0-0	2-1	0-0	1-3	0-5	1-1	0-1	2-1	1-1	4-1	1-1	0-0	2-0	2-0	0-0
Boston United	1-2	1-2	■	1-2	3-1	0-0	0-2	0-1	0-3	3-1	2-0	3-5	0-0	0-0	0-1	1-1	2-2	2-1	2-2	1-2	0-3	1-0
Bromsgrove Rovers	4-1	1-1	2-1	■	1-2	2-2	3-0	1-1	2-2	3-0	1-2	1-2	0-0	0-1	2-3	4-0	0-0	2-2	3-2	1-0	1-0	1-0
Dagenham & Redbridge	2-2	2-1	1-0	1-1	■	5-1	3-1	1-2	3-2	1-2	6-1	4-1	5-1	4-4	0-1	1-2	0-2	1-0	1-1	5-1	1-2	1-1
Farnborough Town	2-5	2-1	4-0	1-1	1-4	■	6-1	3-2	2-2	0-0	2-1	0-3	2-3	1-0	1-1	1-2	0-1	3-2	1-1	0-3	0-2	2-1
Gateshead	2-0	0-4	2-2	0-0	1-1	1-0	■	1-1	1-0	1-0	4-0	0-2	4-1	1-0	0-1	0-0	1-2	3-1	1-1	0-1	4-1	
Kettering Town	1-1	0-1	3-3	3-2	0-0	2-1	2-0	■	1-2	1-0	1-3	2-1	3-3	5-0	2-0	2-0	1-1	2-4	2-1	0-1	0-4	3-0
Kidderminster Harriers	0-1	1-0	0-2	1-0	0-1	1-5	3-3	0-0	■	2-1	1-0	5-3	2-0	1-1	0-2	2-1	2-1	2-1	0-0	1-3	1-4	1-1
Macclesfield Town	1-1	1-0	2-1	0-2	1-1	1-2	1-0	1-0	1-1	■	0-1	1-2	1-1	1-2	4-1	1-0	1-1	1-0	1-1	1-1	1-1	
Merthyr Tydfil	2-2	1-1	0-3	1-1	0-2	1-3	1-1	2-1	4-3	1-2	■	3-0	0-3	1-1	0-0	1-1	4-0	1-1	0-2	1-5	1-4	1-1
Northwich Victoria	1-2	3-1	3-3	0-1	1-1	3-0	0-0	2-2	0-1	1-3	1-2	■	3-2	0-1	1-2	1-3	1-0	1-1	1-3	1-0	0-0	0-1
Runcorn	0-1	1-3	1-2	2-1	1-0	1-4	4-2	2-2	0-0	1-2	2-3	0-1	■	0-3	0-2	2-1	3-1	3-0	4-4	2-3	2-1	1-0
Slough Town	1-4	1-1	3-0	1-3	2-0	3-1	1-0	3-0	3-1	2-1	2-1	0-4	1-1	■	2-1	2-3	2-0	4-2	2-3	0-1	1-1	3-0
Stafford Rangers	0-0	3-2	0-0	3-4	0-1	2-2	2-1	2-4	0-1	1-0	0-1	1-0	0-1	1-0	■	0-0	2-1	4-3	1-1	0-0	1-0	0-1
Stalybridge Celtic	1-0	1-1	2-1	0-1	0-3	2-0	2-1	0-0	2-2	2-1	2-2	0-6	0-0	0-0	1-0	■	3-3	0-0	1-2	3-0	2-2	1-1
Telford United	2-1	0-0	0-1	0-1	0-1	6-3	1-0	3-1	1-1	3-1	5-0	1-0	2-1	1-1	0-0	0-2	■	0-1	0-3	3-3	2-3	1-0
Welling United	2-0	0-3	2-2	4-2	0-2	3-1	1-1	0-0	1-0	5-0	1-5	3-2	2-1	1-2	1-4	1-3	■		2-2	1-1	2-2	0-3
Witton Albion	1-1	0-0	2-0	1-1	2-2	1-1	1-3	4-2	2-2	1-1	3-1	1-3	0-3	1-1	2-5	2-0	2-1	0-1	■	1-2	2-2	1-2
Woking	0-2	0-1	3-0	0-2	1-1	4-1	1-4	3-2	1-5	4-0	0-2	1-0	4-0	1-2	0-3	2-1	3-2	1-0	1-2	■	0-3	0-0
Wycombe Wanderers	0-2	2-0	3-3	4-0	1-0	1-1	2-1	1-2	1-1	0-1	4-0	1-0	5-1	1-0	2-2	4-0	4-0	3-0	2-1	0-0	■	5-1
Yeovil	1-0	2-1	2-1	2-2	0-3	5-2	1-3	2-1	2-2	1-1	0-1	1-1	4-0	5-1	2-0	1-1	1-0	1-0	2-0	4-1	3-0	■

GM VAUXHALL CONFERENCE 1992/93
LEAGUE TABLE FINAL

Team	P	W	D	L	F	A	Pts
Wycombe Wand.	42	24	11	7	84	37	83
Bromsgrove Rovers	42	18	14	10	67	49	68
* Dag'ham & R'bridge	42	19	11	12	75	47	67
Yeovil Town	42	18	12	12	59	49	66
Slough Town	42	18	11	13	60	55	65
Stafford Rangers	42	18	10	14	55	47	64
Bath City	42	15	14	13	53	46	59
Woking	42	17	8	17	58	62	59
Kidderminster Harr.	42	14	16	12	60	60	58
Altrincham	42	15	13	14	49	52	58
Northwich Victoria	42	16	8	18	68	55	56
Stalybridge Celtic	42	13	17	12	48	55	56
Kettering Town	42	14	13	15	61	63	55
Gateshead	42	14	10	18	53	56	52
Telford United	42	14	10	18	55	60	52
Merthyr Tydfil	42	14	10	18	51	79	52
Witton Albion	42	11	17	14	62	65	50
Macclesfield	42	12	13	17	40	50	49
Runcorn	42	13	10	19	58	76	49
Welling United	42	12	12	18	57	72	48
Farnborough Town	42	12	11	19	68	87	47
Boston United	42	9	13	20	50	69	40

* 1 point deducted

Champions : - Wycombe Wanderers
Relegated : - Farnborough Town & Boston United

Diadora League Premier Division — Season 1992/93

	AYL	BAS	BOG	BRO	CAR	CHE	DUL	ENF	GRA	HAR	HAY	HEN	KIN	MAR	STA	STN	STE	SUT	WIN	WIV	WOK	YEA
Aylesbury United		1-0	2-0	6-1	3-2	1-4	0-2	1-1	1-2	0-1	1-1	1-1	2-0	0-3	3-2	5-3	1-2	0-4	3-0	1-2	1-0	1-1
Basingstoke Town	1-2		0-0	1-1	0-1	0-0	2-1	4-0	4-0	0-0	1-0	1-1	0-0	2-1	1-2	1-1	0-0	1-1	3-0	1-1	5-0	0-6
Bognor Regis Town	4-5	1-3		3-2	0-6	0-4	2-2	0-6	4-1	1-2	1-2	0-2	3-4	1-5	2-6	0-0	1-1	1-1	0-1	2-0	2-2	1-4
Bromley	1-2	1-0	3-0		0-4	2-2	2-2	0-5	2-3	1-3	1-3	1-0	0-2	0-1	1-3	4-1	1-2	1-1	1-2	3-0	0-2	1-0
Carshalton Athletic	1-0	0-0	2-2	0-2		1-1	2-2	1-2	2-1	1-1	1-1	3-1	3-0	3-2	3-5	2-1	3-1	2-1	1-3	3-1	1-1	1-1
Chesham United	2-1	2-1	6-1	0-0	5-1		4-0	0-1	3-2	2-2	1-0	4-0	2-1	4-3	2-2	1-0	7-1	7-0	1-0	2-1	3-1	3-0
Dulwich Hamlet	0-1	0-0	2-2	1-1	1-7	1-4		1-2	2-0	1-2	2-1	2-1	1-1	0-5	2-0	0-2	0-2	0-0	5-0	0-1	0-1	
Enfield	3-1	4-1	6-2	2-0	2-1	0-1	1-2		2-1	0-1	2-3	0-2	2-2	1-4	0-2	4-1	1-0	1-0	6-0	4-0	3-0	4-1
Grays Athletic	2-1	3-2	2-1	4-1	2-2	2-0	0-0	3-2		2-1	1-0	0-0	1-1	1-2	3-0	1-1	2-1	1-3	0-0	2-1	2-0	3-0
Harrow Borough	2-3	0-0	2-0	0-2	2-4	0-3	1-1	1-0	0-0		2-2	1-1	2-0	2-5	3-6	2-2	3-1	4-3	0-0	0-0	4-1	3-0
Hayes	4-0	1-3	2-0	3-3	0-4	1-3	0-0	0-1	1-1	2-2		1-1	2-3	2-1	0-0	4-0	0-1	2-2	7-1	2-1	4-2	0-0
Hendon	1-1	0-0	1-0	1-1	1-2	2-1	2-1	0-0	0-1	1-2	2-0		1-0	0-0	2-2	1-1	1-2	1-1	2-0	1-1	1-1	3-3
Kingstonian	7-1	1-1	0-0	2-2	0-2	0-1	2-2	2-3	1-0	2-1	1-1	2-4		2-0	1-3	3-1	0-2	0-1	3-0	0-1	2-0	2-0
Marlow	3-4	0-0	1-2	2-2	0-5	1-4	0-1	1-1	1-1	1-2	3-0	1-1		1-1	5-2	2-3	1-1	0-2	5-1	3-2	1-2	
St. Albans City	1-0	4-1	2-1	4-0	3-2	1-1	3-1	0-0	2-1	1-2	1-0	2-1	2-0	5-1		2-2	2-1	0-1	2-1	3-0	7-2	1-1
Staines Town	1-4	0-1	3-0	2-3	0-3	0-2	1-1	2-2	6-0	1-0	0-1	3-3	1-0	1-4	2-1		2-2	1-1	3-0	1-2	0-1	2-0
Stevenage Borough	1-3	0-2	4-1	0-1	3-2	1-0	2-4	0-3	6-1	0-0	1-2	4-1	2-0	2-0	1-2	1-2		1-0	0-1	1-0	1-1	2-0
Sutton United	4-0	1-0	0-0	3-1	3-1	0-1	2-0	3-2	1-1	2-1	1-2	0-2	1-1	2-1	3-2	2-4	1-1		5-2	3-0	2-0	2-2
Windsor & Eton	2-3	1-0	2-2	0-1	1-4	2-5	2-2	1-3	3-3	0-1	2-3	1-2	1-0	1-2	0-3	3-1	2-4	0-3		1-1	1-2	0-2
Wivenhoe Town	2-1	3-2	4-1	1-0	0-4	0-4	0-1	0-4	0-2	3-0	3-1	2-0	2-3	2-1	0-2	1-1	0-0	1-3	2-0		1-0	1-3
Wokingham Town	0-2	3-1	1-3	1-1	2-2	0-0	3-1	0-3	2-0	1-1	5-0	2-2	0-4	2-2	1-3	2-2	3-0	3-3	3-1	2-0		2-2
Yeading	2-1	1-2	2-1	0-0	1-1	1-2	0-2	3-5	2-3	4-0	1-2	1-3	1-2	0-0	1-2	0-1	2-2	4-0	1-0	0-0	2-4	

DIADORA PREMIER DIVISION 1992/93
LEAGUE TABLE FINAL

Team	P	W	D	L	F	A	Pts
Chesham United	42	30	8	4	104	34	98
St. Albans City	42	28	9	5	103	50	93
Enfield	42	25	6	11	94	48	81
Carshalton Athletic	42	22	10	10	96	56	76
Sutton United	42	18	14	10	74	57	68
Grays Athletic	42	18	11	13	61	64	65
Stevenage Borough	42	18	18	16	62	60	62
Harrow Borough	42	16	14	12	59	60	62
Hays	42	16	13	13	64	59	61
Aylesbury United	42	18	6	18	70	77	60
Hendon	42	12	18	12	52	54	54
Basingstoke Town	42	12	17	13	49	45	53
Kingstonian	42	14	10	18	59	58	52
Dulwich Hamlet	42	12	14	16	52	66	50
Marlow	42	12	11	19	72	73	47
Wokingham Town	42	11	13	18	62	81	46
Bromley	42	11	13	18	51	72	46
Wivenhoe Town	42	13	7	22	41	75	46
Yeading	42	11	12	19	58	66	45
Staines Town	42	10	13	19	59	77	43
Windsor & Eton	42	8	7	27	40	90	31
Bognor Regis Town	42	5	10	27	46	106	25

Promoted : -
Relegated : - Staines Town, Windsor & Eton & Bognor Regis Town

HFS Loans League Premier Division Season 1992/93

	ACCRINGTON STANLEY	BARROW	BISHOP AUCKLAND	BUXTON	CHORLEY	COLWYN BAY	DROYLSDEN	EMLEY	FLEETWOOD TOWN	FRICKLEY ATH.	GAINSBORO' TRIN.	GOOLE TOWN	HORWICH	HYDE UNITED	LEEK TOWN	MARINE	MATLOCK TOWN	MORECAMBE	MOSSLEY	SOUTHPORT	WHITLEY BAY	WINSFORD UNITED
Accrington Stanley	■	2-0	0-0	2-2	3-1	3-1	4-1	6-1	1-0	1-1	0-1	3-0	2-1	1-1	2-0	1-1	2-0	1-1	2-2	2-2	2-0	1-3
Barrow	2-0	■	4-3	3-2	2-1	5-0	3-0	0-1	2-0	1-2	2-2	4-1	1-1	2-1	1-2	3-1	1-0	0-3	2-2	0-2	0-1	0-0
Bishop Auckland	0-0	2-1	■	0-0	5-0	1-1	2-0	2-1	0-1	0-3	2-2	1-1	1-0	3-0	1-0	1-0	0-1	2-2	4-0	1-3	3-2	2-2
Buxton	0-1	0-4	0-3	■	2-3	1-0	1-2	3-0	0-3	2-0	2-3	2-1	2-2	2-1	2-1	1-5	1-1	4-1	6-1	0-2	0-0	2-3
Chorley	0-1	1-1	0-0	1-1	■	4-2	2-0	1-3	2-1	1-2	1-0	1-5	2-2	3-3	2-1	0-6	1-1	1-2	4-2	1-6	1-4	0-4
Colwyn Bay	1-0	2-3	1-2	7-3	1-0	■	3-0	2-1	3-1	0-1	3-0	4-2	4-2	2-4	2-3	2-2	3-1	0-1	2-1	2-4	4-4	2-3
Droylesden	3-3	1-3	1-1	0-0	2-2	1-1	■	1-2	1-1	2-1	0-2	1-0	1-3	1-0	0-1	1-3	2-0	0-1	1-4	2-5	1-2	0-4
Emley	0-3	1-1	2-3	1-1	2-1	1-1	1-3	■	4-3	2-0	0-2	1-2	5-3	1-5	5-5	4-1	2-2	1-2	2-0	0-4	2-1	1-2
Fleetwood Town	0-2	2-2	0-1	0-2	1-1	1-2	1-6	3-1	■	1-1	1-2	3-1	-	1-2	3-0	3-1	2-3	1-2	3-2	1-2	2-2	1-2
Frickley Athletic	3-2	2-1	3-0	2-0	2-1	1-0	0-1	3-1	1-2	■	4-0	3-0	2-1	1-1	1-2	0-0	1-0	2-0	2-1	2-5	3-0	1-2
Gainsborough Trinity	0-2	1-0	1-1	1-2	1-1	2-1	2-1	1-0	1-0	0-1	■	3-0	2-2	2-0	1-4	0-1	2-4	2-3	1-1	1-1	7-1	3-1
Goole Town	0-5	1-0	1-0	0-2	0-2	3-1	1-2	0-0	0-0	1-3	1-4	■	1-2	1-1	0-1	2-3	0-4	2-8	1-1	0-5	5-1	2-4
Horwich	2-2	0-2	2-1	3-0	2-1	0-2	2-1	1-3	2-1	3-1	2-0	3-1	■	3-5	1-1	0-3	2-4	0-1	5-2	1-1	3-3	2-0
Hyde United	2-6	2-2	3-1	2-2	4-0	3-1	2-1	1-0	3-1	0-0	7-2	3-3	4-1	■	2-4	1-2	2-0	2-2	4-2	1-1	2-1	3-3
Leek Town	3-1	2-2	2-3	5-1	3-0	1-4	2-1	2-0	4-1	4-0	1-2	6-1	0-0	3-3	■	0-1	6-0	0-0	3-3	1-0	3-0	0-0
Marine	2-0	2-2	2-0	1-3	1-0	2-1	2-1	2-0	2-0	2-0	2-1	6-3	3-0	3-1	1-1	■	2-2	0-3	1-0	2-1	3-1	2-0
Matlock Town	1-2	0-1	1-5	1-0	3-1	1-1	2-2	2-1	0-1	2-1	3-3	3-2	0-1	1-2	1-0	0-6	■	0-3	1-5	1-2	3-3	
Morecambe	2-0	3-1	2-1	2-1	2-0	2-0	7-4	4-2	3-0	3-4	1-1	2-3	3-3	1-1	1-1	2-2	3-1	■	0-2	4-2	0-0	
Mossley	0-5	1-2	3-1	2-3	1-4	1-4	0-1	1-2	2-0	1-2	2-1	0-0	1-4	1-2	0-4	0-3	0-0	1-0	■	0-2	5-0	2-4
Southport	2-2	3-0	1-0	2-1	7-1	2-0	3-0	1-2	5-0	2-1	0-0	3-0	3-2	1-0	0-0	0-0	3-0	1-1	3-0	■	1-0	0-1
Whitley Bay	1-1	1-1	1-4	2-0	2-2	2-4	5-0	2-0	0-1	3-2	3-0	2-0	0-1	1-0	0-2	1-5	2-3	0-3	1-1	1-5	■	0-3
Winsford United	2-0	1-4	2-0	1-1	0-1	3-2	5-2	5-1	2-0	1-1	1-0	3-0	3-1	1-0	2-0	5-1	0-0	2-0	1-0	1-2	6-0	■

HFS LOANS PREMIER DIVISION 1992/93
LEAGUE TABLE FINAL

Southport	42	29	9	4	103	31	96
Winsford United	42	27	9	6	91	43	90
Morecambe	42	25	11	6	93	51	86
Marine	42	26	8	8	83	47	86
Leek Town	42	21	11	10	86	51	74
Accrington Stanley	42	20	13	9	79	45	73
Frickley Athletic	42	21	6	15	62	52	69
Barrow	42	18	11	13	71	55	65
Hyde United	42	17	13	12	87	71	64
Bishop Auckland	42	17	11	14	63	52	62
Gainsborough Town	42	17	8	17	63	66	59
Colwyn Bay	42	16	6	20	80	79	54
Horwich	42	14	10	18	72	79	52
Buxton	42	13	10	19	60	75	49
* Matlock Town	42	13	11	18	56	79	47
Emley	42	13	6	23	62	91	45
Whitley Bay	42	11	8	23	57	96	41
Chorley	42	10	10	22	52	93	40
Fleetwood Town	42	10	7	25	50	77	37
Droylesden	42	10	7	25	47	84	37
Mossley	42	7	8	27	53	95	29
Goole Town	42	6	9	27	47	105	27

* 3 points deducted

Promoted : - Southport
Relegated : - Mossley, Goole Town

Beazer Homes League Premier Division Season 1992/93

	ATHERSTONE UTD.	BASHLEY	BURTON ALBION	CAMBRIDGE CITY	CHELMSFORD CITY	CHELTENHAM T.	CORBY TOWN	CRAWLEY TOWN	DORCHESTER T.	DOVER ATHLETIC	GLOUCESTER CITY	HALESOWEN TOWN	HASTINGS TOWN	HEDNESFORD T.	MOOR GREEN	SOLIHULL BORO'	TROWBRIDGE T.	V.S. RUGBY	WATERLOOVILLE	WEYMOUTH	WORCESTER CITY
Atherstone United		0-1	1-1	2-4	3-1	1-1	0-2	2-1	0-1	0-0	2-1	1-1	2-3	4-2	4-3	4-2	0-1	1-0	4-4	1-0	1-0
Bashley	2-1		0-1	1-1	5-3	1-3	1-1	1-3	0-2	2-1	0-3	4-3	2-1	0-1	6-1	2-0	1-1	2-0	3-0	2-0	1-0
Burton Albion	1-1	2-0		2-0	2-0	0-3	1-2	3-1	4-0	0-0	0-3	1-1	0-0	1-5	1-2	0-2	4-2	1-2	0-2	2-0	1-1
Cambridge City	0-3	1-1	1-0		3-1	0-3	1-2	6-4	3-1	1-2	6-3	0-3	0-0	3-1	4-4	1-3	3-2	2-1	2-1	3-2	0-0
Chelmsford City	2-1	2-3	1-3	1-1		1-1	3-4	2-1	4-2	1-1	3-1	1-0	2-0	0-2	2-0	0-0	2-2	2-0	2-2	2-2	2-0
Cheltenham Town	2-2	1-2	0-0	2-0	5-1		0-1	3-2	3-1	1-1	4-0	2-1	0-1	1-1	1-0	1-3	1-0	1-0	5-0	2-2	4-1
Corby Town	2-3	5-2	1-1	1-0	2-0	3-0		3-0	2-2	1-0	1-1	1-1	1-1	2-2	2-0	2-2	0-0	1-3	3-1	4-0	1-2
Crawley Town	1-1	3-0	2-2	0-0	3-0	0-0	2-3		5-1	2-1	2-1	3-0	2-1	2-1	1-1	2-1	2-0	2-0	1-1	2-2	4-0
Dorchester Town	0-1	1-0	2-1	5-0	3-0	2-0	1-1	2-3		0-1	1-1	1-0	0-1	2-2	0-0	1-4	1-3	0-1	2-3	0-1	2-1
Dover Athletic	2-0	3-2	3-0	5-0	1-0	0-1	2-0	0-0	3-0		2-0	1-1	2-1	2-1	2-0	1-0	4-0	1-1	2-0	2-0	1-1
Gloucester City	4-0	1-1	1-3	2-3	1-2	1-5	0-1	1-1	1-0	1-1		3-1	6-2	1-3	2-2	1-1	2-4	1-0	1-1	1-1	4-0
Halesowen Town	2-2	3-1	1-2	1-0	1-2	2-1	1-0	4-1	2-2	1-1	2-2		0-2	0-1	5-1	3-1	0-1	4-0	2-2	2-1	3-2
Hastings Town	0-0	0-0	3-0	1-1	1-1	2-1	1-2	2-0	3-2	1-1	0-1	1-4		1-2	1-0	5-1	0-0	1-2	0-2	5-2	1-1
Hednesford Town	1-1	4-1	3-0	1-1	3-2	1-1	1-0	4-2	3-1	0-1	1-2	0-3	3-2		5-1	0-1	2-1	2-0	3-1	1-1	1-3
Moor Green	1-1	1-2	1-4	3-5	3-1	0-2	3-3	1-0	1-2	0-1	6-0	2-0	3-0	1-2		0-1	2-1	1-2	0-2	3-1	2-3
Solihull Borough	5-0	0-1	2-2	0-0	1-2	1-1	0-1	2-2	1-0	1-2	1-3	2-3	1-1	3-0	3-2		4-0	1-0	2-1	4-2	2-1
Trowbridge Town	1-1	3-3	1-4	1-4	1-0	3-3	1-0	1-1	3-1	0-1	1-2	1-1	4-1	3-2	3-2	1-3		4-2	3-2	3-0	2-1
VS Rugby	1-1	1-2	0-1	2-0	0-1	0-5	1-2	1-2	4-1	1-1	0-1	1-3	1-1	1-2	2-1	3-3	2-3		1-0	1-1	1-0
Waterlooville	1-0	0-2	0-1	2-1	1-2	1-2	1-1	3-0	6-1	0-4	1-1	1-1	0-2	1-0	2-1	4-2	1-0	3-1		2-1	0-0
Weymouth	1-3	0-0	1-0	2-0	2-3	0-1	0-3	1-1	1-2	2-3	1-5	2-1	1-0	0-3	0-1	1-2	0-3	1-3	2-1		2-2
Worcester City	2-1	3-0	0-0	2-1	2-2	2-4	2-1	1-2	1-4	1-2	2-0	1-0	2-0	0-0	0-2	2-0	3-0	0-5	0-0	1-3	

BEAZER HOMES PREMIER 1992/93
LEAGUE TABLE FINAL

	P	W	D	L	F	A	Pts
Dover Athletic	40	25	11	4	65	23	86
Cheltenham Town	40	21	10	9	76	40	73
Corby Town	40	20	12	8	68	43	72
Hednesford Town	40	21	7	12	72	52	70
Trowbridge Town	40	18	8	14	70	66	62
Crawley Town	40	16	12	12	68	59	60
Solihull Borough	40	17	9	14	68	59	60
Burton Albion	40	16	11	13	53	50	59
* Bashley	40	18	8	14	60	60	59
Halesowen Town	40	15	11	14	67	54	56
Waterlooville	40	15	9	16	59	52	54
Chelmsford City	40	15	9	16	59	69	54
Gloucester City	40	14	11	15	66	68	53
Cambridge City	40	14	10	16	62	73	52
* Atherstone United	40	13	14	13	56	60	50
Hastings Town	40	13	11	16	50	55	50
Worcester City	40	12	9	19	45	62	45
Dorchester Town	40	12	6	22	52	74	42
Moor Green	40	10	6	24	58	79	36
VS Rugby	40	10	6	24	40	63	36
Weymouth	40	5	10	25	39	82	23

* 3 points deducted

Promoted :- Dover Athletic
Relegated :- VS Rugby & Weymouth

105

HFS LOANS 1st DIVISION 1992/93
LEAGUE TABLE FINAL

Bridlington Town	40	25	11	4	84	35	86
Knowsley United	40	23	7	10	86	48	76
Ashton United	40	22	8	10	81	54	74
Guiseley	40	20	10	10	90	64	70
Warrington Town	40	19	10	11	85	57	67
Gretna	40	17	12	11	64	47	63
Curzon Ashton	40	16	15	9	69	63	63
Great Harwood Town	40	17	9	14	66	57	60
Alfreton Town	40	15	9	16	80	80	54
Harrogate Town	40	14	12	14	77	81	54
Worksop Town	40	15	9	16	66	70	54
Radcliffe Borough	40	13	14	13	66	69	53
Workington	40	13	13	14	51	61	52
Eastwood Town	40	13	11	16	49	52	50
Netherfield	40	11	14	15	68	63	47
Caernarfon Town	40	13	8	19	66	74	47
Farsley Celtic	40	12	8	20	64	77	44
Lancaster City	40	10	12	18	49	76	42
Shepshed Albion	40	9	12	19	46	66	39
Congleton Town	40	10	7	23	58	95	37
Rossendale United	40	5	5	30	50	126	20

Promoted : - Bridlington Town & Knowsley United
Relegated : - Rossendale United

Shepshed Albion have transferred to Midland Combination

BEAZER HOMES LEAGUE MIDLAND DIVISION 1992/93 SEASON
LEAGUE TABLE FINAL

Nuneaton Borough	42	29	5	8	102	45	90
Gresley Rovers	42	27	6	9	94	55	88
Rushden & Diamonds	42	25	10	7	85	41	84
Barri Town	42	26	5	11	82	49	79
Newport AFC	42	23	8	11	73	58	75
Bedworth United	42	22	8	12	72	55	71
Stourbridge	42	17	9	16	93	79	71
Sutton Coldfield	42	17	9	16	82	78	68
Redditch United	42	18	6	18	75	79	66
Tamworth	42	16	11	15	65	51	64
Weston-super-Mare	42	17	7	18	79	86	61
Leicester United	42	16	9	17	67	67	59
Grantham Town	42	16	9	17	60	73	54
Bilston Town	42	15	10	17	74	69	52
Evesham United	42	15	8	19	67	83	50
Bridgnorth Town	42	15	7	20	61	68	50
Dudley Town	42	14	8	20	60	75	46
Yate Town	42	15	5	22	63	81	43
Forest Green Rovers	42	12	6	24	61	97	33
* Hinckley Town	42	9	11	22	58	89	30
King's Lynn	42	10	6	26	45	90	29
Racing Club Warwick	42	3	7	32	40	88	29

* 1 point deducted

Promoted : - Nuneaton Borough & Gresley Rovers
Relegated : -

Barri Town have transferred to Welsh Abacus League

BEAZER HOMES LEAGUE SOUTHERN DIVISION 1992/93 SEASON
LEAGUE TABLE FINAL

Sittingbourne	42	26	12	4	102	43	90
Salisbury City	42	27	7	8	87	50	88
Witney Town	42	25	9	8	77	37	84
Gravesend & N'fleet	42	25	4	13	99	63	79
Havant Town	42	23	6	13	78	55	75
Sudbury Town	42	20	11	11	89	54	71
Erith & Belvedere	42	22	5	15	73	66	71
Ashford Town	42	20	8	14	91	66	68
Braintree Town	42	20	6	16	95	65	66
Margate	42	19	7	16	65	58	64
Wealdstone	42	18	7	17	75	69	61
Buckingham Town	42	16	11	15	61	58	59
Baldock Town	42	15	9	18	59	63	54
Poole Town	42	15	7	20	61	69	52
Fareham Town	42	14	8	20	67	65	50
Burnham	42	14	8	20	53	77	50
Canterbury City	42	12	10	20	54	76	46
Newport I.O.W.	42	9	16	17	44	56	43
Fisher Athletic	42	8	9	25	38	98	33
Andover	42	7	9	26	42	99	30
Dunstable	42	5	14	23	42	92	29
Bury Town	42	8	5	29	46	119	29

Promoted : - Sittingbourne
Relegated : - Gosport Borough

Andover have left the League

106

DIADORA LEAGUE 1st DIV. 1992/93
LEAGUE TABLE FINAL

Hitchin Town	40	25	7	8	67	29	82
Molesey	40	23	11	6	81	38	80
Dorking	40	23	9	8	73	40	78
Purfleet	40	19	12	9	67	42	69
Bishops Stortford	40	19	10	11	63	42	67
Abingdon Town	40	17	13	10	65	47	64
Tooting & Mitch. Utd.	40	17	12	11	68	46	63
Billericay Town	40	18	6	16	67	61	60
Wembley	40	14	15	11	44	34	57
Walton & Hersham	40	14	12	14	58	54	54
Boreham Wood	40	12	14	14	44	43	50
Maidenhead United	40	10	18	12	45	50	48
Leyton	40	11	14	15	56	61	47
Whyteleafe	40	12	10	18	63	71	46
Uxbridge	40	11	13	16	50	59	46
Heybridge Swifts	40	11	9	20	47	65	42
Croydon	40	11	9	20	54	82	42
Chalfont St. Peters	40	7	17	16	48	70	38
Barking	40	10	8	22	42	80	38
Lewes	40	9	10	21	34	80	37
Aveley	40	9	7	24	45	87	34

Promoted : - Hitchin Town, Molesey & Dorking
Relegated : - Lewes & Aveley

DIADORA LEAGUE 2nd DIV. 1992/93
LEAGUE TABLE FINAL

Worthing	42	28	7	7	105	50	91
Ruislip Manor	42	25	12	5	78	33	87
Berkhamstead Town	42	24	-8	10	77	55	80
Hemel Hempstead	42	22	12	8	84	52	78
Metropolitan Police	42	22	6	14	84	51	72
Malden Vale	42	20	9	13	77	54	69
Chertsey Town	42	20	7	15	84	60	67
Saffron Walden	42	19	10	13	63	49	67
Newbury Town	42	14	18	10	53	51	60
Hampton	42	16	11	15	59	59	59
Edgware Town	42	16	10	16	84	75	58
Egham Town	42	16	9	17	60	71	57
Banstead Athletic	42	14	13	15	67	51	55
Leatherhead	42	14	11	17	66	61	53
Ware	42	12	11	19	68	76	47
Witham Town	42	10	16	16	54	65	46
Tilbury	42	12	8	22	55	101	44
Barton Rovers	42	9	14	19	40	66	41
Hungerford Town	42	11	8	23	37	93	41
Rainham Town	42	9	10	23	56	80	37
Harefield United	42	10	7	25	37	72	37
Southall	42	7	7	28	43	106	28

Promoted : - Worthing, Ruislip Manor & Berkhamstead Town
Relegated : - Harefield United & Southall

DIADORA LEAGUE 3rd DIV. 1992/93
LEAGUE TABLE FINAL

Aldershot Town	38	28	8	2	90	35	92
Thame United	38	21	11	6	84	38	74
Collier Row	38	21	11	6	68	30	74
Leighton Town	38	21	10	7	89	47	73
Cove	38	21	8	9	69	42	71
Northwood	38	19	11	8	84	68	68
Royston Town	38	17	8	13	59	42	59
East Thurrock United	38	17	7	14	69	58	58
Kingsbury Town	38	15	9	14	62	59	54
Hertford Town	38	14	10	14	61	64	52
Flackwell Heath	38	15	6	17	82	76	51
Tring Town	38	12	11	15	59	63	47
Hornchurch	38	11	13	14	53	52	46
Horsham	38	12	7	19	63	72	43
Epsom & Ewell	38	10	11	17	52	67	41
Bracknell Town	38	7	13	18	52	94	34
Clapton	38	8	7	23	46	74	31
Camberley Town	38	8	7	23	37	72	31
Petersfield United	38	6	12	20	36	90	30
Felt. & Houns. Bor.	38	5	4	29	47	119	19

Promoted : - Aldershot Town, Thame United & Collier Row
Relegated : - Peterfield United

SCOTTISH NON-LEAGUE REVIEW

This is an annual publication which first appeared in 1988, reviewing the previous season. From humble beginnings, this has progressed to an annual 60 pages, including several of photographs in each of the past two issues. All the final league tables and all cup results for the three 'senior' Leagues (Highland, East and Southern) and each of the six Junior regions are included. Additionally, many smaller, local amateur league tables are included. Add to this a look at the programmes issued and new books on the non-league game in Scotland and you have the most comprehensive look at the growing non-league scene in Scotland.

Although the first annual REVIEW is long since sold out, all the others are still available :

Review of 1988/89 £1.00
1989/90 £1.30
1990/91 £1.30
1991/92 £2.00
1992/93 £2.00

Each issue costs an additional 28p postage (any excess sent will be refunded). A special offer to readers of this publication gives you all five for only £7.00 post free.

As well as publishing the annual REVIEW, there are also several other publications on the subject available. These include the annual SCOTTISH NON-LEAGUE FOOTBALL HISTORIES which have over 40 pages of articles on clubs and associations from the past as well as some from the present. Volume One is now sold out but Volumes 2 and 3 are available at £1.50 each (plus postage) or £3.00 post free for the two.

The statistics of the Ex-Scottish League clubs are documented in PAST MEMBERS OF THE SCOTTISH LEAGUE. Part One of this covers all the clubs beginning with the letter 'A' (giving their grounds, League membership details, cup wins, colours worn and their Scottish League record, including dates and results of every match played, individually detailed against every other club). This costs £2.00 plus 24p postage. A S.A.E. will give you details of future parts which will all be available during the course of the 1993/94 season. Various books by other publishers (many of these independently published with small print runs) are also available, again in receipt of an S.A.E.

If you wish to purchase any of the above books, please make any cheques or postal orders payable to STEWART DAVIDSON, and write to :

12 WINDSOR ROAD, RENFREW   PA4 0SS

TEAM TALK

The F.A. officially-approved monthly magazine of Non-League Football.

Now in its 3rd Year - covers all levels from Conference to County Leagues and cup competitions.

80-pages per issue priced £2.20 from all good newsagents.

SPECIAL OFFER

12 Issues delivered directly to your home for just *£24.00*

write to :

Team Talk (dept SG-NL)
24A Queen Square
North Curry
TAUNTON
TA3 6LE

72 St. Peters Avenue, Cleethorpes, DN35 8HU, England
24hr orderline (0472) 696226
Faxline (0472) 698546

VHS only

ALL PRICES INCLUDE POSTAGE
UK : 1st Class Letter Post
Overseas : Airmail Post

10% DISCOUNT ON ALL ORDERS IN EXCESS OF £60.00

UK - FORMAT VIDEOS (Suitable for UK, Europe & Australasia)

OFFICIAL HIGHLIGHTS OF THE SEASON

All priced : £14.49 UK ; £17.99 Overseas *(including postage)*
(All videos last 90 minutes unless shown otherwise)

1992/93

Arsenal	Aston Villa	Chelsea
Everton	Leeds United	Liverpool
Manchester City	Manchester United	Norwich
Sheffield United	Sheff. Wednesday	Tottenham Hotspur
Ipswich Town	Newcastle United	Blackburn Rovers

1989/90, 1990/91 & 1991/92

Arsenal	Aston Villa	Chelsea
Everton	Leeds United	Liverpool
Manchester City	Manchester United	Tottenham Hotspur
	Glasgow Rangers (Scottish)	

1988/89

Arsenal	Aston Villa	Chelsea
Everton	Liverpool	Manchester City
Manchester United	Nottingham Forest	Tottenham Hotspur
	Glasgow Celtic (Scottish)	

Order From : **The Soccer Bookshelf (Dept SG10)**
72 St. Peters Avenue, Cleethorpes, DN35 8HU, England
Pay By : **Cash/Cheque/Postal Order or**
Credit Card : **Access/Mastercard/Barclaycard/Visa/Amex**

10% DISCOUNT ON ALL ORDERS IN EXCESS OF £60.00

Order from the small selection below or send for our full list of over 150 books

THE COMPLETE RECORD SERIES

This highly-acclaimed series of Hardback Club histories contains a full record of results, line-ups, attendances, scorers, managers and players' profiles. Each priced £16.95 unless otherwise shown. Postage UK +£3.50; Overseas +£5.50; Air +£10.50

Accrington Stanley 1894-1962; Arsenal 1886-1992; Aston Villa 1874-1992; Blackburn Rovers 1875-1990; Blackpool 1887-1992; Burnley 1882-1991; Celtic 1888-1992; Chelsea 1905-1991; Coventry 1883-1991; Crystal Palace 1905-1989 (£14.95); Derby County 1884-1988 (£14.95); Everton 1878-1993; Exeter City 1904-1990; Grimsby Town 1878-1989 (£14.95); Hull City 1904-1989 (£14,95); Leyton Orient 1881-1990; Manchester City 1887-1993; Middlesbrough 1876-1993; Millwall 1885-1991; New Brighton (£12.95); Newcastle United 1882-1990; Nottingham Forest 1865-1991; Oldham Athletic 1907-1988 (£14.95); Oxford United 1893-1989 (£14.95); Q.P.R. 1882-1993; Saints (Southampton) 1885-1987 (£15.95); Spurs 1882-1993; West Bromwich Albion 1879-1993; West Ham United 1895-1993; Wrexham 1873-1992; York City 1922-1990.

OTHER TITLE

THE BREEDON BOOK OF FOOTBALL LEAGUE RECORDS

An excellent book containing every result and league table.

Hardback Price £16.95   Postage : UK + £3.50 ;   Overseas + £5.50 ;   Airmail + £10.50

Order From : **The Soccer Bookshelf (Dept SG10)**
72 St. Peters Avenue, Cleethorpes, DN35 8HU, England
Pay By : **Cash/Cheque/Postal Order or**
Credit Card : **Access/Mastercard/Barclaycard/Visa/Amex**

Other Supporters' Guides : -

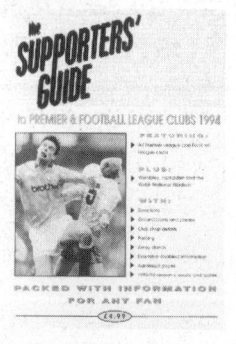

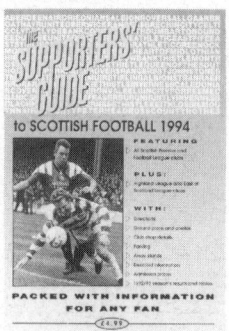

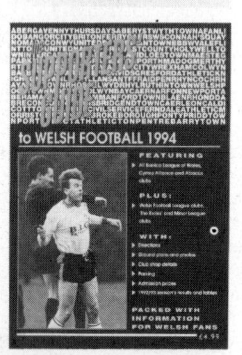

THE SUPPORTERS' GUIDE TO PREMIER & FOOTBALL LEAGUE CLUBS 1994

Featuring :
- all Premier League clubs
- all Football League clubs
- all 3 British National Stadia
+ 1992/93 season's Results & tables

120 pages - price £4.99 - post free

THE SUPPORTERS' GUIDE TO SCOTTISH FOOTBALL 1994

Featuring :
- all Scottish League clubs
- all Highland League clubs
- all East of Scotland League clubs
+ Results, tables

96 pages - price £4.99 - post free

THE SUPPORTERS' GUIDE TO WELSH FOOTBALL 1994

Featuring :
- all Konica League of Wales clubs
- all Cymru Alliance clubs
- all Abacus clubs
+ 'The Exiles', Minor League clubs & 1992/93 season's results and tables

96 pages - price £4.99 - post free

order from : -

**SOCCER BOOK PUBLISHING LTD.
72 ST. PETERS AVENUE
CLEETHORPES
DN35 8HU
ENGLAND**